T0090156

Mom's Idea

By

Nathan Smith

Order this book online at www.trafford.com
or email orders@trafford.com

Most Trafford titles are also available at major online book retailers.

Printed in the United States of America.

ISBN: 978-1-4269-3744-6 (sc)

ISBN: 978-1-4269-3745-3 (hc)

ISBN: 978-1-4269-3766-8 (e-book)

Library of Congress Control Number: 2010909188

*Our mission is to efficiently provide the world's finest, most comprehensive book publishing
service, enabling every author to experience success. To find out how to publish your
book, your way, and have it available worldwide, visit us online at www.trafford.com*

Trafford rev. 8/31/2010

 www.trafford.com

North America & international
toll-free: 1 888 232 4444 (USA & Canada)
phone: 250 383 6864 ♦ fax: 812 355 4082

CHAPTER 1

Let me start right in the middle. It was Christmas in the inner city, but there was not much joy in the air. I was living in the center of the inner city near the jail. It was the sort of place, I quickly found out, where you never walked on the sidewalk at night, and during the daylight, you never talked to passers by. If you're lucky, no one would rob and beat you. Of course you had to be white for it to be that way. It wasn't that it happened everyday; it was that everyday I lived in fear of it happening. When it did happen, it was terrifying and shocking. I feared every day.

My roommates were all mentally ill like I was. But living there gave us the chance to live somewhere where it was possible to go without taking our medications. The landlady didn't care as long as the disability benefits kept coming in regularly. She would cash our checks, give us the amount left over after rent and board, and never complained about what we did as a treatment plan. Back then I believed that the government would keep sending my check no matter what, because I had been diagnosed with schizophrenia. I found out a few years later that even if someone was mentally sick, as I was, and not taking medications and seeing a doctor regularly, that the government would claim that I no longer needed their financial help.

We were living there, drinking every day, and the landlady provided breakfast and dinner. I was eventually thrown out of a nearby bar for being intoxicated, but there were still plenty of drinking establishments who would serve me. I also did a good amount of drinking at the house where we all lived because it was too expensive to always drink at bars.

One Sunday I was walking back around the comer from where I lived, and a big man, a black man, wrestled me to the ground and went through my pockets. I didn't have much. When he had taken everything, fortunately for me, he left me alone to get up and walk away.

The roommate I had in my room, not just in the house, was a very tough old black man. We came to an understanding that if I did not speak to him while we were both in the room, he wouldn't bother me. Four of the men living there were white, but everywhere else for square miles around, the neighborhoods were all black. We stood out like sore thumbs. By the experiences I had, I figured that the muggers believed they never could be found in the huge numbers of black people in the area. It would be impossible for them to be caught. I also came to believe that there was no conscience in the minds of our tormentors, because we were the ones who were trespassing on the inner city harmony and peace. There had to be something wrong with us to live there.

Mom and her husband came down into the city to give me some Christmas presents that year. When they got here, they couldn't find me right away. Mom had a cigarette lighter, which was all she had for light to find me by. She walked up the stairs to my room. I was not there, but in the dark, a voice shouted out, "What are you doing here?" She was scared, but really didn't know how much danger there was around her.

When they finally found me, I didn't want the presents, and I asked her to go back home and leave me. The months of not taking my medications and drinking had affected my brain, so I was rude and didn't appreciate their love and support. When the time came, I would finally ask for their help to move out of there to someplace safer.

For years I had accepted on faith that I should take my medications and that also I should stop drinking. I usually took the medications as prescribed, but I did not have as much luck with the drinking. I needed to experiment to see if I could drink and exist without medications.

I went out early one Sunday morning to attend church. It was a half-mile through the southern end of the inner city, where rows and rows of black families lived. The church service started at 6:00 AM, so it was quite early. As I neared the middle of one particular block, a figure started towards me. I didn't think anything was wrong, but then he kept on coming toward me; I got really scared. He reached out and grabbed my arm. I swung around twice, with him trying to rob me. Finally his hand broke free, and I started running as fast as I could to the end of the neighborhoods. He started after me. I was still scared. I ran as fast as I could, until finally I was past the hospital into a white neighborhood. He stopped and went back, presumably because he was a afraid he'd be discovered. It was a truly good feeling to know that I was safe. It was stupid to go out that early, even to go to church, but I kept going, hoping Jesus would save me. The man never approached me again.

After a few weeks, the damage to my mental state from the robbery started to heal. I thought this was all there was, and that I was free. I was wrong about that though, which I will include later in this account.

Despite the trouble appearing to be over at least briefly, things were, in general, very desperate. I wasn't doing anything positive in my life, just drinking and watching the days go by. Every month I would walk five miles to where my father worked, I would ask him for twenty dollars, and he would give it to me. I did this at the end of each month when my check would be gone, to tide me over until the beginning of the next month. If I drank at home mainly, this would do ok, but the drinking really ate up my small monthly income.

Mom and her husband went to Italy after Christmas to see the Roman ruins and the lovely cathedrals. In my mental state, worsened by the crimes I had suffered, I began to blame my family, including my mother, for my situation. Day after day, my mind deteriorated. In addition to the paranoia, I kept hallucinating very strange things. The birds and insects chirping hour after hour became an audio hallucination that there were white women who were looking for me, but somehow they had been taken in and captured by the next door neighbor. He was raping them in my mind, and the chirping was the sound of his thrusts into them and back out again. I thought there was a big problem.

I called the police and reported it. I was not in contact with reality. I think the police must have been trained to deal with mental illness, because nothing became of it, or at least not yet.

CHAPTER 2

My mind kept deteriorating such that soon I began to believe that my parents were also trying to kill me. I thought they were living it up while I was suffering in this difficult situation. They had put me into the mental hospital a few years before. I was horrified. It was so painful emotionally to think that I was ill in my mind and that I would never be successful. I had even tried suicide because of this after my second hospitalization. Fortunately, I didn't have the courage to go all the way, and only swallowed an amount of medications that was not lethal. This was the crowning glory of my absolute misery and discouragement. It had to be true, I thought; why else would I be there, except if they were trying to kill me. I was the ugly duckling who ruined the family image. All of this, of course, was not true.

I even called the FBI and told them my parents were trying to kill me.

I'm sure now that this only meant to them that I was mentally ill and needed a psychiatrist.

All through these times my mother kept hoping and wanting a better life for me. She hadn't put me down there in the inner city, and neither had the rest of my family. It was truly bizarre how my mind was getting sicker and sicker. I was so miserable that I didn't even know I was miserable. To land there, in the city, I had left a nice apartment and day clinic behind, simply because there were two rules there which I didn't want to follow. First we had to take medication as prescribed, and secondly, no drinking.

You can imagine that someone without the usual responsibilities of life, while feeling sorry for myself due to the brain disease which I had, really liked to drink. And it was true to a point. When I was drunk, I didn't think about the terrible disease; I didn't think about failure. I couldn't perceive what my real situation was and how I could be happy if I accepted it.

Today, however, I played golf. The weather was beautiful. I had on great looking golf clothes and had an enjoyable round. After that I came to Mom's house and had a little lunch. What has happened to get me to this point from that ghastly situation down in the inner city? Let's say, it was mom's idea. She was the only one who kept pushing and prodding to make me realize how much good there was in the world and how I could live properly and enjoy life. Part of this was taking medications every day and abstaining from alcoholic beverages. I never thought I could do it, but today I have three years and almost seven months without a drink, and I take my medications.

Let's go back again to those bitter times, talk about what happened to me, retrace the steps I took that landed me first in the inner city, and see what finally led me to where I am today.

Drinking was denial, so one day I took all the dollars I had in my pocket and went to the city instead. This one decision started the real downward spiral that got me to the inner city. I walked the streets that afternoon; soon afternoon turned into night. The only thing I could do was to walk around the city, all night long and hope for morning to come fast.

The next day I inquired about where the homeless shelters were. The nicest one I could find was open from about 5:00 PM until 7:00 AM. Everyone was lined up for a block or so waiting for the doors to open. There we could take a shower. After that, I wanted to go out back and smoke cigarettes until dinner.

Just before the dinner bell though, a fight broke out in the smoking area. Two black men were standing; one stood behind the other, and the one behind held a large knife at the other's throat. Dark, red, blood was coming slowly out of his neck; I went inside as calmly as I could. I had called the police before, but for some reason, this time I was in spell from witnessing this violence. It was so bad that I couldn't even go to the people working there to report it. A day later, I left my overcoat inside, a remnant of the civilized life behind me. I saw someone wearing it when I came back indoors. I didn't dare mention it. He was welcome to it. If he could wear it, there's no telling what he would do if discovered and challenged. I just walked calmly by.

The next day I called my brother, and he tried to get me back in the supervised housing. They said if I went into the hospital for a month I could return, so I went in. The hospital didn't seem as bad after what I'd been through, but it wasn't too long before I started to become as I was before.

After a few days in the hospital, I started to feel uncomfortable. It was, as usual, a locked ward. It was located in the city, but it was like an oasis. They had free soft drinks and black coffee, and they allowed smoking on the ward. Except for the mornings, I smoked and watched television.

After a couple of weeks, one of the nurses took me off the ward and drove me around in her car. I don't know why she did this, and it had never happened to me before. After driving around for an hour, she brought me back to the ward. Nothing happened though, nothing changed inside me, and eventually I was back to where I was before. The days slowly went by until we made plans for my return to the supervised apartment. I didn't really want to be there though. I needed to experiment some more with not taking medications and drinking.

After a few days I walked out to the bus line, and I was gone. I knew that there would be no coming back after all of that, the hospitalization. When I arrived downtown, I went to the nearest bar and sat down. I ordered a beer, and soon it was sliding down my throat. The cool liquid tasted good. Soon, after a few beers, I started to feel good too. The situation I was in faded, and the alcoholic euphoria was there for a while again. I then, as it started getting to be late afternoon, I got up from the stool and headed for the park opposite the homeless shelter. I had plenty of money.

At the park, I sat down. After a few minutes, a big black man started to approach me; I thought at first he was just lonely and wanted to talk. As he came nearer though, he pulled out a large knife. He put the knife right up against my neck and lowered me down on the bench. I intuitively knew not to resist or fight. After I was prone, with him keeping the knife at my throat, he went through my pockets until he found my money. He took it and was gone. So now I was broke again. I had nothing left but the soup they gave out for dinner, with not even enough money for a pack of cigarettes.

I couldn't go back. They wouldn't take me. The next day I went to the soup kitchen that served breakfast. After a morning meal of pork chops and green beans, I asked a staff member there if they knew of anyone who would take in boarders. I still had my social security disability check, and if I could find anybody who would be my representative payee, I could rent a room. Since I was considered at risk of misspending my money on alcohol, it was the rule of social security that someone else must cash my check for me. I could not cash it myself. The lady there at the soup kitchen said she knew of a lady who would be my payee and give me room and board for two hundred dollars a month. That gave me a hundred dollars left to spend where I would.

I was told I could wait there at the soup kitchen after closing, and she would contact the lady who was to be my new landlord.

Her name was supposed to be Rose. I waited for about an hour, and then a big busted, slightly overweight black woman with a big smile came through the door. She smiled and held out her hand saying, "You must be Timothy."

She explained everything, and part of it was that I had to take my medications. After this orientation, she drove me over to the house. There were two of the four people who lived there at home. Rose introduced us. She said then just to wait there, and in the morning we would go to social security to arrange for my check to stop coming to the supervised apartment but instead to her.

I borrowed a pack of cigarettes from one of my housemates and just sat around until dinner smoking them, one after another. It was good to be there, even though I was again required to take my medications. At least I didn't have to go to an adult day care center and make crafts or learn more about my illness. It was horrible back there at the apartment. Every day I was reminded that I was ill, and not like everyone else. I was free here to do whatever I liked during the day. Rose told me that, just like the other fellows, I was free to get into any sort of trouble I could as long as I didn't bring any of it back to the house. No guests, no alcohol, and no drugs were allowed on the premises.

Around five thirty, a medium height black man with big muscles and not much fat on him came in carrying food for our dinner. His name was Mark, and he was Rose's assistant. I remember thinking that he was strong enough to handle any of us if we were having a problem. Once, later on, he grabbed someone there, sat them down, and made them take medications. I didn't have a problem taking them after witnessing that event.

The foods were rather simple and inexpensive. Noodles and hot dogs with fruit punch to drink, were the daily menu. I was very hungry that first day, despite breakfast early that morning about 8:30 am. I didn't know then, but I lost fifty pounds eating this stuff over the next two years. It must be a blessing of the poor. They can't afford rich foods, so they don't get fat.

As I lay my head on the pillow that night, with me on the opposite side of the room from Charles, my roommate, I inhaled the sense of a wonderful, new adventure.

CHAPTERS 3

I was there for real; there was no going back. I was in the inner city, miles from everything that I knew. It was all mine, thanks to Mark and Rose. Tomorrow was a big day; Rose and I would get my check squared away, and we'd be established.

I awakened to the sound of Mark opening the front door carrying in more food, except it was breakfast this time. He hollered rise and shine. So while the eggs were crackling on the stove, I dressed and went downstairs. I only had one shirt and one pair of pants.

Everyone was seated at their places and took their morning medications. I had to wait until after our trip that morning to buy some of my own at the pharmacy.

After breakfast I had several hours or so before the time we would go. About an hour and a half later, mid morning, Rose came in laughing and carrying on with the other boarders. She genuinely seemed to like us and the job she had made for herself.

I sat and watched television while Mark did the dishes and Rose talked to the other boarders about how they were doing.

Soon we were off. The social security office was jam-packed, so we took a number and sat down. After an hour's wait, we were called. Rose quickly signed the payee papers, and we were told that it would take fifteen days to process. Rose said that I could stay and pay back the money for rent over a few months.

On the way back, she bought me a carton of cigarettes that I would pay back also.

I was there to stay. The afternoon I spent smoking cigarettes and going back to my old apartment to pick up my few things there.

CHAPTER 4

My parents didn't really complain, but I'm sure they were disappointed. They simply said I was to stay there and that I should keep it. They, especially Mom, said that I must like it, since it took so much effort to find it.

It was still hard to feel good while the rest of the family was living it up. They seemed so cavalier about it all while I was suffering down there. There had been no crime yet. I thought it was quite nice too after I gave it some attention. After I adjusted from the relatively plenty to this place which was mine, life was enjoyable. It sounds strange, and not very ambitious, but I liked it.

In a few weeks I would visit home. My family had worked for every penny they had, and I was awarded disability insurance. That much was mine. I would buy jalopenia cheese and tortilla chips, and the afternoon was complete. While they played golf and went to the swimming pool, I munched my chips and cheese. A fan blew the air around, while an airconditioned clubhouse awaited the golfers. Life was much different between the rest of the family and me.

Later on, I would buy a half pint of bourbon and pour it into a soft drink can so I wouldn't be arrested for public consumption of alcohol. As long as I didn't bring it back to the house, it was ok with Rose and Mark. This was a great relief. Before, at the supervised apartment, there was no drinking, either on or off the premises. It was amazing how important alcohol became after it was prohibited. I used to spend hours brooding not being allowed to drink alcohol under any circumstances.

One thing for sure about the present was that, like in the supervised apartment, I had no responsibilities.

I thought the check would come forever, but I was to find out later that I had to be seeing a psychiatrist and taking medications to be eligible for these benefits.

CHAPTER 5

One of the guys there with Mark and Rose went to a program in the city. He was black, and his parents lived somewhat near Rose and Mark's. It was very similar there to what I had left, except mine had been in a white neighborhood. I suppose you could say that the program I left had better real estate, but the funding and organization were the same.

One day I went to the soup kitchen for lunch, and right behind me in line were a white man and woman; he had long hair and a beard. We started talking, and I mentioned that psychiatry was doing great things and seeing one would help him. I didn't think for a minute that he would really go and see one.

I didn't see him for three weeks, and then Rose announced that we had a *new member to her boarding house.* Then in walked Mark, not her boyfriend, but the man I had spoken to in the soup kitchen line. Incredible! He must have gone to see a psychiatrist. Rose announced that he had just been discharged from the mental hospital.

Rose left, and very soon after she did, Mark with the beard and long hair became very, very angry at me. Apparently he did not like what the psychiatrist had done. He had never expected to be hospitalized as insane. He was upset. He didn't like the suggestion. As weeks went by, he finally cooled down and finally expressed that it was a good thing that had happened. He was tired of being poor, and this was a relief.

Another time, one of the boarders came in the door all covered with dust, dirt, and grass clippings. He had been in a terrible fight with the next-door neighbor. Knowing him as I did, I thought it was all his fault, and it probably was. Soon after that, the police came in. I showed the officer a hole in the plaster wall where Carl, the fellow in the fight, had punched his fist. For some strange reason, nobody was arrested. I suppose that was because Carl was mentally ill, so they declined to arrest him.

I used to go to the 8:30 am mass at the Catholic Church almost every day. Religion seemed to fill a hole my life. I could hope for anything. Mark, the boyfriend of Rose, made a comment that I still don't understand to this day. He said that the church next door had saved me. I didn't know if he meant that it explained why I was absent from breakfast so much, or it could have been just a general statement recognizing the power of God to save.

My mind was still slowly slipping away though. I could not bear my poverty, and the circumstances around me compared to the rest of my family and my school chums. I was degenerating into a twisted kind of horrible person. I called the police and complained that my father had a gun and that it made him very forceful when he told me to take my medications. I then told them that he had never threatened me with a gun. It was a foolish thing, and only the expertise of the police avoided my father from being deeply hurt by my unfounded statement.

CHAPTER 6

Soon it was time to move. Rose had found a house for less money in a worse neighborhood, right by the city jail. It was at this point where we all (the boarders) started with the plan of not taking our medications. Rose had hired a full time live-in cook who did not make us take our medications. It was at this place where the thefts started which I put down in the beginning of this account.

One night at dinner, things got very desperate. I was in a miserable paranoid delusion most of the time. I made things worse that night when I mentioned to the fellows that my father's company owns a farm where we put out targets and shot at them. One of my brothers and I were there. We were young teenagers I guess, and we enjoyed it. Somehow though, in relating it, my mind leapt into the thought that that there was a man in the woods just behind the targets who was bound by my father and left to be killed by our teenage target practice.

It was terrible to accuse my own father of such a horrible crime. Thank God I never called this in to the police. Somehow

I avoided this. I don't know how. Years later when I think of this, it still upsets me and it is disturbing to remember. The crimes committed to me left my mind badly twisted, as well as my untreated illness. I lashed out at the only important thing that I had in this world, my family. I discussed this with my psychiatrist recently, and he assured me that this sort of thing was common to schizophrenics and not to worry about it. Even though he said that, and I believe him, the memory of that terrible night still seems scary.

CHAPTER 7

It is very reassuring to know from my psychiatrist that my mind had blown this out of proportion. He said that many people have had a similar problem and done ok. In a way, it was like dad had given me a reason, to accept my disease and its treatment. If none of this had ever happened, I wouldn't want to take the medication and stay sober. It was like a spiritual gift, making sure that I take the medication, and nothing wrong will happen. There is no way the simple expression would have weight alone; this made me sure I'd take it for fear of letting those horrible feelings take over.

It was at this point that the episodes I described in the beginning of this story took place. After all that went on, someone, probably the cook, asked people in from the neighborhood. I was in my room one day, and two women came in. They were black, like the cook. I said hello, and they started hitting me in the head and asking for money. In truth I had none, but they kept on. Finally, after fifteen minutes of this, they left. I was, to say the least, relieved.

I brought it up at a house meeting, and Rose said not to let anyone in the house. In a few days one of the women came back, and somebody let her in again. I was sitting in a chair in the dining room, and the woman brandished a knife or letter opener, but didn't say anything. There were other people there, some of the boarders, and apparently she didn't want any one to know what was going on. To anyone else but me, it looked like she was just playing with the knife, especially because she didn't threaten verbally. I knew she was doing this for my benefit, as if to say that she wanted money.

One evening later on, I went down to the bar district about a fifth of a mile from the house. I sat there awhile sipping my pint of beer. Then I asked the barmaid if she would like to marry me. She walked over to her boss. So I approached them both, and her boss said to leave and not come back. I was fairly drunk, and the alcohol had lowered my inhibitions. The pint wasn't the first drink I'd had that day.

A week or two later, I was going to a 6 AM church service. Before I made it to the church though, I was arrested. Later, I found out it was for breaking and entering. After two weeks in jail, I saw a judge who acquitted me and said that if I wanted to, I could sue the government, but I declined. That was stupid. I needed money and turned it down. Sometimes to this day, years later, I regret not suing, but I don't think it will ever happen again. If I had a choice, I'd rather not be arrested again than have a second chance for money.

It was God's gift, and I had turned it down, and I'll probably never have that chance again.

CHAPTER 8

After a while, I thought I would see if mom would take me in again. It was just too rough down there, so I called her, and she said ok. Three weeks went by living with her, and she finally found a place for me to live on my own. It was in a fairly nice section of the city.

The landlord there had a rule that if I was to stay there, I must take my medications. I refused, and he threw me out. Before he did throw me out, I was really getting sick. I called the police saying that the other tenants had captured a woman and were torturing and raping her. I also called the police and told them that I loved Marilyn Monroe and wanted to marry her. I was getting sicker and sicker as the months piled up without medications, and my drinking whenever I could. Everyone knew it but me. So I was homeless again soon enough, and started to hitch hike.

I walked from the neighborhood to the interstate. After an hour or two I got a ride. He drove me west and then north to Pennsylvania where I got out. Not too long after, a Pennsylvania police officer came and arrested me. I was taken to the station, finger printed, and photographed. Then I was shown my cell. There was a big screen television in the jail there that we could watch. I didn't have any cigarettes. That was the worst part of it. There was all sorts of crude graffiti on the prison walls. Some of it was detailed and could even be thought of as art, if you stretched the definition a little. There were all sorts of demons and occult symbols too.

Some days went by, and I remembered my high school government class where they talked about the constitution guaranteeing the right to a speedy trial. I picked up the phone inside the prison and expressed that I was ok, but that they had abused my right to a speedy trial. The next day I was called up to court.

The judge said that the charge was hitch hiking and asked me my plea. I said guilty. I had been hitch hiking, so that was what I said. The judge asked for my father's phone number down in Maryland. After I gave it to her, she called and asked if he would send money to pay my bus fare back to Maryland. It was all arranged. Two police officers drove me to the bus station where I had to wait a couple of hours for the next bus. Dad sent a little extra so I could buy some cigarettes. Finally the bus came.

I remember thinking that the bus trip was long. It was dark too, by the time we arrived at the Baltimore bus station. I only had to wait for about fifteen minutes for dad and his wife to show up. We drove back to the county, and dad said I needed help, and I should go to the emergency ward and go into the mental hospital. That was actually the correct plan. I needed to be stabilized on medication and observed during the transition. Back then I didn't really know that as well as I do now, but I knew it was it was really the best thing I could do. Even though it pained me in my heart and emotionally, I was very respectful and thankful towards my father for helping me.

The hospital emergency ward did some interviews and then I was told to wait. In a couple of hours, I walked out the door. I tried to walk the seven or eight miles to the apartment mother had arranged. When I got near the house a gang of teenagers grabbed me and pushed me to the ground. These boys were white. After they left I limped onward through my pain to the apartment. I did call the police and reported the beating. An officer took notes and then left. I walked to the back door of the old apartment. The door was unlocked. I slowly and painfully made my way to the bed and lay down. It really felt good for an instant, and then the pain returned. It was a relief from walking, but the pain was severe.

In any case, I was soon asleep. I was unaware that I didn't live there anymore and could be arrested for trespassing.

In the morning I got up, stiff and in pain. Without really thinking about it, I decided to walk all the way back to the hospital. This was smart, because after the interviews I was expected to be there, and I would be arrested and taken to the mental hospital. Two or three hours later, I arrived at the emergency room. How I had done it, I don't know. Though in great pain I was able to make the way on foot. Humans are capable of amazing feats if their survival depends on it.

After I arrived, they conducted more interviews, and then I was placed on a stretcher and belted down. That way I had less pain and also couldn't run away again.

People came in and out of the emergency ward. It seemed like forever. Finally some nurse's assistants rolled me out to an ambulance where I was transferred from my stretcher to the ambulance. After about a half an hour for the paperwork to be processed, I was away on another exciting journey.

CHAPTER 9

Once again I had something that was really mine. I had to be careful though, and not let life's inconsistencies turn to harsh make-believe statements against my family. This was another chance to become human again. As it turns out, I was at peace for a time after this, but the old twisted mind eventually returned. For now, I was safe from the criminal element. It was ok that there were criminals in the hospital. There was staff, and they kept the order and worked with those who qualified and were not kept in jail.

My memory is not complete of these months, but I do remember the general appearance of the place. It was the first time I had ever been a patient at a public hospital. Once before, of course, I was in a public hospital for alcoholism, but this one was not focused on that. Alcoholics anonymous meetings were allowed, but the treatment was not centered around alcoholism specifically.

I can recall just one story, but I'm not going to relate that here. It was about a man who was discharged after a few weeks. I don't know where he went.

All in all it was a relaxing hospital stay. The food I thought was ok. The weeks passed by filled by others with complaints about the food. I remember going off the ward every day to walk and smoke cigarettes. The hospital's campus was actually very beautiful. It had lots of trees and a stream. Not all of the buildings were in use; I was told later that only about one third of the buildings were. The rest were boarded up. The architecture was stone and there were a few newer red brick buildings. It seemed that the forebodeing nature of the architecture was fitting for a public mental institution. There was one non-imaginary reason for the foreboding, and that was the iron bars on all of the windows, on both used and unused buildings. They were there to protect the patients from harming themselves or others. The doors to the outside were locked of course, but in the wards they were open. This way the patients had maximum benefit of the therapy and had a chance to make progress. With the mentally ill, progress is very, very slow and sometimes hardly perceptible. They have the best chance of adjusting successfully if they are prevented from indulging in harmful activities.

Every Thursday, people would come to preach the gospel of Jesus Christ to those who wanted it. I had been a churchgoer before. The missionaries were very different though. They sang very folksy, with some of them being rather quite beautiful in their own way, hymns. I believed in God too, so I went despite the folksiness, just to have some peace and feel the love of God. Those nights were very enjoyable, and I thought the missionaries were very good to give us that short time of spiritual refreshment.

I had another group I attended one day a week too, where we focused on substance abuse. I had been an addict who used drugs to avoid life's real challenges, and of course, an alcoholic for the same reasons.

We tried to look at what made us drink and what we could do to stop drinking. Schizophrenics are known to do lots of self-medicating with alcohol. Now needless to say, the alcohol was only a temporary relief. Soon came the headaches of hangovers, and the symptoms of schizophrenics do return, seemingly worse than before. It is somewhat common for schizophrenics to do this. The prescription medication does a much better job on reliving tension and paranoid feelings than the comparably crude alcohol use.

My mother knew this, and she always suggested that I go to the psychiatrist and take my medication. She urged me to be sober, to abstain from any alcohol relief also. The rest of the family swept me under the carpet to be sicker and then of course die. I don't blame them, and I understand now that it's nothing personal. They simply realized the enormity of the task of rehabilitating a chronically ill schizophrenic. The odds were against me. I believe that the four years of abstinence from alcohol, which I now have, are the exception rather than the rule.

Also success stories like mine are, as the scientific community would put it, a phenomena. These phenomena are explained as spiritual experiences occurring to a patient who has been diagnosed as hopeless with no chance of recovery. When the rest of the family gave up, which was perfectly reasonable, Mom pushed on, never allowing the worst to set in. Some people are born as exceptional, and mother was that. There were times I resented some of her efforts, but they were always correct and beneficial. In this way, I was, because I was sick, very fortunate to have her as a relative.

It's also a fact that even if a patient takes his medication regularly as prescribed, indulging in alcohol reduces the effectiveness of the medication. I've heard stories from alcoholics who were seeing psychiatrists report that if they were drinking, the doctors refused to see them. It apparently was the case that heavy alcohol use masked the patient's mind, preventing an accurate analysis.

Architecturally, the hospital was lonely and bleak. The staff always tried to keep seasonable decorations up though. It was mostly built just after World War Two out of cinder black, although some parts of the hospital were built way before the post World War Two buildings. I heard that these were used to chain patients to the wall as a medical treatment.

Nowadays, psychiatric treatment has advanced to a more humane approach to mental disease. First of all, there were only a few types of medication before, and these usually had very serious and notable side effects. The new medications don't have as severe side effects and help treat the problem better. The symptoms go down with the new medication, and the patient can live a relatively normal life.

Some days I would stay out for several hours. I could walk off hospital grounds and visit the town. I just had to submit where I was going and when I'd be back. They usually approved of everything I asked for. I had been there for several months and the staff trusted me. There really was next to nobody outside during the weekends. It was strictly nature, me and cigarettes.

I would usually sit at the base of one of the very tall, old trees on the hospital grounds, but I still felt uneasy sometimes. I would feel how wonderful the day was, sitting beneath a tree. The next few minutes I would feel like I had to get up. The ground was hard, or roots were protruding from the ground at the base. Then I'd walk around and look at everything.

There was a building that was unlocked on weekends. It was the medical building that took care of all physical ailments except those requiring a hospital's attention. In the lobby were two or three vending machines where the few with money could by candy bars and soft drinks. In the wintertime, the heat was left on so that any patient who was cold outside could come in and warm up. There were usually, but not always, some patients there at the medical center. Many times I asked my fellow patients for a cigarette. Some times they gave me one.

Chapter 10

On weekdays, those who qualified could walk up to the canteen staffed by volunteers, and there were plenty of seats inside for the wintertime or for those who wanted to watch television there. I used to watch the television, because I had no cigarettes to smoke outside. There were a bunch of us who didn't have cigarettes and begged. After the first half hour, no one gave out cigarettes to anybody if they could help it. There were just too many people. The volunteers sold coffee and candy. They also served loose, single cigarettes for a quarter.

After about four months, I was scheduled to be discharged. I was to go into my second supervised apartment, located a few miles outside of the city in a small town. Here I felt safe. There were no thieves walking up and down the streets. I spent a few days here each week, then the rest of the week back at the hospital. They liked to take their time and be sure everything was ok.

I remember my roommate there. He was a longshoreman by trade. Longshoreman loaded and unloaded the big ships in the nearby harbor. Some of these ships were from across the ocean. He seemed like a wheeler-dealer to me. He had a stack of pornographic videos, and once he brought a girl back to the apartment who was a stripper at a bar he frequented. The idea of supervised housing didn't appeal to him. As soon as possible he was trying to move out.

We had inspection every Saturday. A counselor would come and see that we cleaned the apartment. The counselor made a rule, too, that we had to smoke on the balcony and not inside the apartment. Things went along pretty well until the cold weather came along, and then we started smoking inside. The counselor just turned the other way because it was so cold. We still opened the balcony door for about an hour each day to freshen the place up though. After about forty-five minutes, the apartment was warm again.

Pretty soon, Randy, the longshoreman, left. I had the whole place to myself. I didn't dare drink there for fear I'd lose my place. My life was boring. I didn't talk much, and after program hours, I would just sit and watch television, or just sit.

My medicine was the old variety, so my legs jittered, and I was usually uncomfortable. My psychiatrist after a while started to reduce my dosage to make me more comfortable. She was an Indian lady from the orient, not native American. She was a kind woman. Because of my analysis, she insisted that I take my medication by injection. This made sure I took it. I received one shot each month. It was a time-released injection and lasted the entire month.

CHAPTER 11

I got a new roommate soon. He was a Jewish fellow who worked as a landfill inspector for the county. His job was to see if all the garbage was disposed of sanitarily.

For the life of me, I couldn't imagine why he was mentally ill. When I asked him, he muttered something about taking a woman's bra off in public. I think that's what he said. Morris was his name. He was a lady's man around the program. He soon started bringing women from the other apartments over for soft drinks or coffee.

It had been a long time since I was with a woman. I started to imitate him. If he could do it, so could I. The only problem was that there were a limited amount of female clients around. So I just brought one woman over at first. Lucy was her name. At first she resisted, but after a half an hour of coaxing, she removed her clothing and began to remove mine. This was really nice. It had been a long time. Her skin felt so smooth, and her small bosom jiggled with our movements. A few minutes passed, and it was over. After that, I asked another woman over. I didn't want to settle with just one. I was surprised that they all, even the most conservative looking, wanted sex as much as I did. Sex became a way to relive the boredom.

After a few more months, another roommate was assigned to us. He was also Jewish, but very different from Morris. His name was Mike. All he wanted to do, he said, was to take LSD and look at cartoons on television.

Soon it was spring, and I signed up for the softball team. We practiced, and then had a schedule of games with other rehabilitation centers. The coach's name was Harry. We had a few practices where Harry would hit balls to us in the field and we would throw to first base. When I batted, I could not hit it long enough when I tried to hit it hard. Therefore I tried just to meet the ball. The ball would clear the infield and land short of the outfield. This worked fairly well.

Soon I was assigned to be the pitcher. I loved to try and throw it very hard underhanded. Then the games started.

We had about a five-and-five record when it was all over. We really had fun. It was great that there were programs such as this for people as miserable as I. We weren't just left on our own to sink or swim. I was so glad that my wrongs were verbal and not otherwise. I felt like maybe after therapy for a little over a year, I was capable of forgetting those miserable days in the city. God only knows why after about two years there, I was again ready to depart. I failed to realize that the result could be as bad as before, and it was.

My doctor consented to change my disability insurance payment from my mother's to my own name. That meant I could cash my own check. We did all the paper work, and my doctor made me promise not to take off, but to stay in the apartment and keep taking my medication shots. With the first check I received, I opened up a bank account and was off to the city. It was a different part of the city, but the scenario was fairly much the same. The first thing I did was to buy a big bottle of bourbon and some soft drinks to mix with it. This was great. I even had a small television set, compliments from mom. Then I found a place to stay.

It was a small room with a tiny refrigerator, a bed, a bedside table and two large windows. This was heaven. I was on my own again, only this time I could cash my own check. I paid the nominal rent and utilities payments to the landlord. The rest was all mine. After a couple of days I was completely inebriated. A few months went by, and all I did was drink alcohol, smoke cigarettes, sleep and eat.

There was nobody white around for days sometimes, except a few of the other tenants and the landlord. Outside of the apartment building, almost everyone who was there was black. I sat a lot on the front steps of the apartment building.

One day, a young black woman walked by. Out of sheer boredom and jolliness, I asked her if she wanted to come in for a drink. It was only neighborly; there weren't any white people around, so it was one of them or nobody. She did, and I poured. After a while, she told me that she had walked all over the city, and that someone had tried to stab her. She asked me if I had any money. I gave her the three dollars and change in my pocket. Then she left. Well that was certainly something. A few more days went by, and she came back. Her name was Stacey. This became sort of routine. She did not ask for money again right away.

There was a Catholic soup kitchen just down the road from the apartment. I got in line one morning. If I ate there, it meant I would have more money to spend on liquor. As I was coming out after the meal, a tall black man said that there was a lady there looking for a man. He said she was stupid to look at a soup kitchen because everyone was broke, or they wouldn't be eating there. That was certainly true, because the food was not too good, and you really had to be poor to find eating there desirable. He pointed to her, and I shrugged.

In any case, I walked over and asked her if she wanted to visit me in my apartment. She said yes. The feeling I got from her was very sexual. We got to my room, and I closed the door. We sat there quietly for a minute, and then she asked me if I was ready and started to take off her shoes. At this cue, I started taking off my clothes.

When I had gotten them off, she said that it was going to cost me. She took off her blouse and let the round, warm tits hang there above her abdomen. She stayed about five more minutes. Then she asked for a piece of fruit, a sweater, and some underwear. I gave her an orange, an old sweater, and a pair of my underwear. After that, she asked for cash. I gave her ten dollars. From the look on her face, I felt like ten dollars was very disappointing to her. She was only there for about ten minutes. When she was leaving, she said that if I wanted her to come back, she would come; all I had to do was to give her a date and time, and she'd be there. Because she wanted money, I told her I didn't want her back. She said fine and left.

Word must have been getting out about me in the neighborhood. I was walking back from the grocery store, and near my room a voice called out in the middle of the sidewalk for me to wait; she needed to talk to me. She said it was Stacey. I knew she didn't look like Stacey, but I waited anyway, and she caught up to me. Closer now, I could see she definitely wasn't Stacey. I didn't say anything but just started walking again after she caught up.

She came inside, and in a minute she had become entirely naked. I was starting to wonder about it, especially with the money they wanted for sexual favors. I said I didn't want to have sex. She started begging and pleading emotionally. She sat in my lap, I fully clothed and her entirely naked. She pressed her bosom, which was a rather nice shape and size, up to me, and emotionally pleaded for me to make love to her.

Inside, my desire was on fire, but I kept it to myself and said no, I didn't want to have sex. This went on for a few minutes until I could convince her to clothe herself. I even offered her money to leave. I figured that was what it was all about. No sex, leave, and I'd give her twenty dollars. She asked for thirty; I was trying to make her promise to go. At thirty she said she would go. Just before leaving though, she said how about forty. I told her right then and there that she had agreed to leave for thirty, and would she please go. Soon she left, and the door was shut. Alone at last was I. This whole thing had gotten out of hand.

CHAPTER 12

A few weeks later, I was walking by the elementary school when my old girlfriend, a white woman about five years younger than me, passed by. I called out her name. At first she didn't know who it was. Then she cried out my name, Timothy, and said how good it was to see me. We talked for a while, and she gave me her address. She lived there with her boyfriend nowadays and her two girls of elementary school age.

The last time I saw her, her first child was an infant. We had broken up just before then. I think it was because the psychiatric medicine I needed had the side effect of not being able to impregnate a partner. She had tried with me for a couple of years and eventually set off to have a family with someone else.

In a few days I went by her place. She said I was always welcome there. Her boyfriend worked, and she had all day to herself while the kids were in school. Our favorite thing was to drink coffee, smoke cigarettes, and listen to the radio. We even discussed marriage, and she said she wouldn't leave her boyfriend who had fathered her children. He wouldn't marry her, but she didn't want to leave him.

She still smoked pot too, so it was really good for me that she declined my proposal. It might have been impossible or very hard to get her to quit. She said maybe she would marry me after menopause. These years I would now turn her down if she reached menopause and asked me to marry her. Now that I'm sober and taking my medications, it doesn't look like a very good thing for me. Things go better being with Mom. With what little money I have, I cannot really afford a woman. It's all I can do to keep up my wardrobe and play golf. With a woman like her I would lose all of that.

Today I bless the fact that we didn't have children also. When I grew up, I went to an expensive summer camp in Maine, private schools, and was a member of a posh country club. I would be doing well just to keep them in clothes. I also believe now that sex is for having babies, and it would be a sin to have a partner this late in life merely for the thrill.

A few days later, the real Stacey came back. I didn't answer the door bell, so Stacey came around to my window and yelled up that she would find me somehow, even if she saw me in the street, and there would be no getting away. This bothered me, but it was nothing compared to what happened next.

Stacey came back again, and out of vague fear I let her in. She drank my bourbon and slept a lot. Some times she came late at night. I kept letting her in. This was a mistake, because the more I resisted her, the greater the possibility became that she would not return.

I tried ignoring the bell again. Unfortunately, it was wired from the front door to a bell with a hammer. It was very loud, so I answered it eventually. She just kept ringing and ringing it. It wouldn't stop. She knew I didn't have money, because she ate the spaghetti with butter that I cooked for dinner, because I didn't have anything else or money to buy something. After a few more months of this, she asked me if I wanted to have sex, I said yes, and we had sex with a condom. After that she left.

This was my second mistake. She came back again and asked me if I had any money I could give her. I said no, which was true. Then she asked me how much money I had in my wallet. I told her I had twenty dollars, which was also true. She said to give it to her. I told her that I needed the money for expenses next week. I looked at her, and suddenly she was holding one of my kitchen knives. She repeated her desire for me to give her the twenty. I started to resist, and she told me to watch out, that she wasn't playing, and that she would cut me. I took her seriously and told her it was ok to take the money.

She left, and as she was walking down the hall from my room, I called out for her to leave my wallet, but take the twenty. She dropped it on the floor. Then I asked her to leave my knife, which she also dropped on the floor as she was leaving. I let her get out of the door, and then I retrieved the wallet and knife.

There was no phone in my room; I couldn't afford one. I thought of walking outside to the phone booth there around the corner, but I thought that maybe she would wait there to see if I was going to call the police; she knew I didn't have a phone. So I let it slip by, and I didn't call the police. I think that she needed the sex act to be able emotionally to rob me. This then was my second mistake. Somehow it must have made her able to think that I owed her money.

The landlord told me before long that I wasn't allowed to have those girls in or I'd be evicted. This was great. It was just what I needed, to have someone help. I knew it was a desperate situation. I told him about the one who robbed me at knifepoint, and he told me it was alright to stay because I promised to take care of the situation.

A few days later, I called dad. He said he wanted to put me up in an apartment away from the scene down there. I don't know how he knew, but he said it was bad for me down there. So we went out apartment hunting. We eventually looked at a real nice one in a better neighborhood. The landlord said, however, that he wouldn't take anyone who was not paying the rent directly. He wouldn't let dad pay for me while I was the only tenant. So we kept looking. —

Recently, I had seen an advertisement for housing discrimination. I didn't know then, but I think what the landlord said was against the law. The next one said the same thing. Dad finally said he would buy a house where he would be my landlord. The prospect of living in a house excited me. We looked at one that was near a grocery store. I didn't have a car, so this was perfect. Dad asked if I liked it, and I said I did. He called a friend of his who worked in real estate to make the arrangements. He paid for it in one payment, and the house was mine. This was really living. I even had my little social security check coming in.

CHAPTER L3

Practically as soon as I was there, I walked into downtown Towson to the bar district. I'd drink there everyday. It left me with no money for groceries. I used to drink the day my check came, right up until there was no money. I used to ask Dad and Mom for money after there was no money. Usually they gave me some.

I lived to drink. The first thing in the morning, I'd pour a glass of wine, if I had it. Other wise it was anything I had. Tequila, bourbon, or beer, it didn't matter.

I used to go to meetings. I had meetings when there would be other alcoholics there with the same problems. We shared our dilemma, and how we overcame or will overcome it. I would usually go to these meetings drunk. I also went there after my money was gone, since they had free coffee and sometimes donuts.

I also kept wondering why I couldn't stay sober. Mom could see my struggling with alcohol. She urged me over and over to stop drinking. Then I couldn't do it.

Also it had been a good long time since I'd seen a psychiatrist or taken medications. Mom also urged me to see a psychiatrist again. She knew that it was not good that I had stopped taking medication; I had a chemical brain disorder. It was nothing to play around with. I was a hard head on both of these. I didn't want to stop drinking, and I didn't want to take my medication. It must have been frustrating for my mom who was unsuccessful at trying to do what was best for me.

There were other family members who had died from cirrhosis of the liver. Most of my family swept it under the rug. Mom, however, never gave up. She kept trying and trying, even though for the longest time she was unsuccessful. She is just a special person that way. She knew that if I could be stabilized on medication and could stop drinking, I would be able to live a normal life. I did not know it then, but boy was she right. I thought my medications didn't help, and that I was not mentally ill. I also thought that it was my God given right to drink if I wanted to. I was so miserable that I couldn't tell I was miserable.

Loneliness overtook me finally, and I got on a bus headed downtown to the nudie bar district. It was expensive too. Back then, in the 1990s, it was twenty-five dollars for a beer. It was not like in the movies. The girls who danced had no clothing on at all. Their entire bosom was showing, and even their pubic areas. I spent about $80 after the beer on the girls, putting a ten or a twenty in their garters. I guess the nudity got the best of me, because I finally asked one of the strippers to marry me. She said yes. We went over to a couch and got it on for about ten minutes. That was it. Soon enough, I was out of the door with just enough change to catch the bus back home about ten miles.

I had gotten the stripper's phone number though. She said to call her in a couple of days. I got home and went to bed. The next day I called her, and she was very cheerful, but she said she was busy. The day after that I called her again, and a man's voice answered. He said that I was not a problem, and he wasn't complaining, but could I please not call anymore. I agreed, and we hung up.

Things seemed, looking back, to be getting a little out of order. The drinking was starting to have obvious effects, which were not very agreeable. One day I got out the neighborhood directory and dialed the number for the baby sitters listed there, but I had no children. It turned out that all the baby sitters were teenagers. I was in my late forties. I apologized then hung up.

Another time I was at a rummage sale across the street. The lady giving the sale had two young daughters. I started telling them how it was wrong to masturbate. Drunk as I was I didn't know what I was saying. The neighbor called the police. I had gone home by the time they got there. But in a few minutes, the police were knocking at the door. I opened the door, wine glass full of wine in my hand. The police were very nice, and they didn't arrest me. Instead they told me if I ever went back across the street to the lady's address, then I would be arrested. Fortunately I was not drunk enough to go back. To this day I have not gone back.

There was another neighbor down the street, who in a conversation mentioned that he was a lawyer. He also told me a tale that was so bizarre I don't know whether I imagined it or he actually said it. He said that in the middle of the night, he went out to the alley and shot someone there. He said the police never questioned him about it. Looking back I wish I had dropped it there. Maybe it was because of the heavy drinking. Nonetheless, I called the police and reported what he had said. Days and weeks went by, and they never arrested him. I think it was very cruel of him to tell me what he did tell me, because it disturbed me mentally. Being ill I was in no mental shape to hear or report something like that.

A few months later, I received a call from a woman, probably African American, asking me if I would give her any information about this neighbor, Bob. She also said that how I answered her question would have an effect on me. This didn't scare me then, but now as I remember, it makes me wonder. Even though it's been a year or more, I worry. I answered her question by saying that I didn't know Bob. She hung up, and I guess that was the end of it. Like I said, today, even though I'm doing everything the doctor said to do, and keeping regular appointments with him and my group therapist, I still worry and feel apprehensive about the call I received from the African American lady. My mind tells me it's been too long ago, and that nothing could happen now. After all this time, it is safe to say nothing more will come of it. My emotions, however, are still in a state of worry about this and other experiences.

CHAPTER 14

A couple of years after moving in to the row home, I was sent a letter telling me I had an appointment to review my case. It was to determine whether or not I was still disabled and thereby qualified for the disability insurance. Without taking it seriously, I let the weeks slip by, and when the appointment came, I did not show up. I had a crazy notion that I would always have the insurance. Soon after that, I received a notice that I was being cut off. I didn't know how I would live.

A few months before this notice, I was drinking in a bar in Towson, where I live. Well, I was sitting there on a barstool, when an older woman came up and suggested that we go in her cab she had waiting out back. It was a short drive to her apartment. When we got to the door, she started saying that I had approached her. She then asked me if I wanted to come in. She had it backwards. I don't know why she said it. Very strange it was.

Upon entering, she poured us each a glass of wine. Then she gave me a grand tour of her apartment. The apartment was nicely decorated, and there was plenty of room. It was an expensive apartment. We went into the living room. She told me that her husband had died, and that she owned a horse farm on the eastern shore of Maryland. I should have left because she was too old for me, but just having some attention from another person was so wonderful. I had lived alone for too long. She was even touching me in the living room. Shortly, we decided to go out. I felt self-conscious because she was older.

We were walking through the parking lot of a different bar located in the shopping mall across the town from her apartment, when four or five men appeared in an out of place, beat up old sedan. She seemed hypnotized by them. I begged her, Margaret that is, to come along now. Eventually she did. There was a gas station on the other side of the parking area. We stopped there to call another cab. She was sitting on the curb, and I asked her if she was all right. Then I picked her up from the curb where she was sitting and put her in the cab. Then I got in, and we were safe from the men.

It was bedtime when we arrived back at her place. I went into the bedroom and sat on the bed keeping my clothes on. A minute or two later Margaret came up completely naked and sat down beside me. I gathered one of her nicely shaped breasts into my hand. Her breast was really quite something too. It was large enough, and its shape was beautiful. We went on like that for a few minutes, and then tried to complete it. For some reason although I lost my stuffiness, I was unable to be with her that way. After this trying, we both went to sleep.

It was a large king or queen size bed, so there was plenty of room for both of us. I awoke however, just after midnight, so I tried watching television in the den. After an hour I decided to leave. Margaret was still asleep, so I left her a note and told her in it that I had to go; it just wasn't working for me.

I had a pair of clip-on sunglasses with me, so I left them there by the note to symbolically represent the difference in our ages. I was young enough to be her son, so these I left were "son" - glasses.

After that I went out and carefully closed the door very gently so she would remain asleep. It was only about one half mile to my house, so I decided to walk it, even though it was late and therefore dangerous. I went home, locked all the doors, undressed quickly, and went to bed.

When I awoke in the morning, I felt embarrassed. Why had I given in to her? Part of my mind answered and said that maybe she was younger than she looked. The rest would say no. I was a little overweight. Perhaps because of this, she thought I was older than I was.

CHAPTER 15

I was drinking and not taking my medication again. Without the meds and with a lot of liquor, my mind wasn't functioning well. One time I was drunk, and I called my congressman and suggested that we all should have elephant meat in the grocery store. After a few weeks of suffering and thinking how strange my request was, I called back and apologized. Another time I called the police and told them how twenty or thirty years ago my father had smoked pot. Later I called the police and told them that my stepfather and the neighbors next door were stealing from me when I wasn't home, and that they were putting a hole in my attic roof. The missing money was undoubtedly spent by me at the local bars.

One of the fellows at my meetings where we helped each other to stay sober told me a strange story. It was bizarre, like that of Bob, the neighbor. I called the FBI, and reported it. It didn't occur to me until later that the reason why he was referred to our group was because of these strange episodes, and that there was no need to go farther. I felt terrible. I had been very hateful and not working with him to stay sober. The result? Even though I went to meetings, I drank to anesthetize the emotional pain of my betrayals. Every time I saw Joe in the meetings, I got this horrible feeling that I was getting very sick and that I was ashamed of what I had done.

I put down here some of my bad experiences to somehow convey how severely alcohol can effect the human mind. I don't think I am a bad person; instead I am a sick person for whom heavy alcohol use has created misery. The world didn't stop because of my sinful speeches. However I was brought to utter psychological ruin because of my insatiable desire for alcohol. I believe that alcohol is the major factor in turning a boy or a girl into a criminal. To an extent, given enough alcohol, it will ruin even the best of people.

Let's get back to some more of these episodes.

There was a friend living near me who I knew from the first supervised living program. I saw him at one of the alcohol meetings, so I went over to his apartment one day, looking for something to do. He had friends over, a man and a woman. They said they needed a place to stay for a few days, and I invited them over. We left and went to my place. They unpacked a little. After about an hour the woman, Joan I think her name was, asked me if she could smoke pot in my basement. I didn't know what to say, so I said yes.

Another half an hour went by, and there was a knock at the door. Nobody ever knocked, so I wondered who it could be. It was the police. They said they had received a call from a neighbor about my guests. The woman left with the police, and the man stayed the night and left in the morning. I was very relieved when it was over, because the woman had asked about pot, and smoking in my basement.

After the man left, I looked in the refrigerator. In the freezer part there were two or three large bags of what looked to be illegal drugs. I didn't open them because I had never seen drugs like that. When I first saw them, I thought they were some kind of food. They weren't mine though, and once I realized what they probably were, I took them out of the freezer and put them in the outside garbage can.

For a while I was worried whether they or someone else would come back for the drugs. The size of the packages was large enough so that, if they were drugs, they were worth a lot of money. I didn't know how much, but I was sure it was a lot. I worried whether they would be disappointed at their loss and threaten me. Now several years later, they still have not come back.

The man and woman worked at the Ramada Inn nearby. The day after they left I called the police and told them where they worked so the police could investigate them. After all those strange conversations, I finally had something real to say.

At one of my meetings for staying sober, there was a guy who was trying to sell drugs at the meetings. He had been coming for a while before I was aware that he was a drug dealer. Because of this, I had his last name and phone number. I called the police. Now it has been a few years, and he never came back. I assume he is still in jail.

There were people begging on the street corners sometimes. One day I asked one of them in. He stayed an hour or so, and then I decided it was a stupid mistake. That guy could be anybody, even a criminal. Thank God when I asked him to leave, he left.

I went back to the bars and as I sat down at one, the manager came over and threw me out. I had begun to notice that things were getting worse. This confirmed it. Pretty soon my money would be gone too. They had after all cut it off on the grounds that I didn't go in for my appointment to have my eligibility updated.

I didn't know what to do, so I went out to the highway and tried to get away out of state and start over.

It soon became dark on the roadway. An older model luxury car eventually pulled over. He took me to a grocery store and bought me a loaf of bread, a jar of peanut butter, and a jar of jelly.

He asked about what was doing, and I told him about Candy, the stripper. I was lucky that this guy was, as far as I knew it, not dangerous. He let me off in Montgomery County, Maryland. I walked and walked until a state police patrolman pulled over, and I told him to please arrest me; I was hitch-hiking, and that was illegal. He said he wasn't going to arrest me, but he would take me to a building where they would refer me to a shelter and the soup kitchens. It was a long night.

There was a woman state police officer at the receptionist office of the building. I sat down and tried to sleep. Before the morning, I told her to read a passage from the Bible. It was the one that says the sick and those in prison are His. Since then I've felt embarrassed that I gave her a passage of the Bible to read. It was unnecessary. I know that it's part of my illness when I'm not taking my medications and drinking. Since then I have noticed through this and other examples that I should keep taking medications and not drink.

In a way I'm sort of glad I had these strange experiences, because now I'm convinced that I need treatment. In the past I was just going to treatment to make others happy, including my mother. She helped steer me in the right direction.

There is only so long that a person can stay sober for someone else. Now I was convinced that I needed to stay sober for myself. It was not like before when I had drinking in the back of my mind, but stayed sober for the doctor and my mother. Now I believe that drinking is not an option.

Mom kept after me over the years to stay in therapy and stay sober. She is a fighter, and she fought for me when I was headed for trouble. The meetings I attended had one saying for this. It was said, and I think truthfully so, that if an alcoholic continues drinking, the best that he or she can hope for is to land in jail, live in a mental institution, or die. Mother was after me, because she wanted to see me live and enjoy life.

It was hard to accept that I could not drink, and that I needed medication. Therefore, I resented my mother for the longest time.

Perhaps it was not resentment, but the idea of being discouraged. It's very hard for a person willingly to accept alcoholism. I'm sure that this kind of problem is common in alcoholics and mental patients. They cannot accept either. Therefore they blame the family. It is common for us to call the police, because we are delusory about what is going on. I just thank my lucky stars that it never resulted in serious violence.

I know a patient from my psychosocial group who, while visiting his parents in New York, tried to stab them. He had to go to jail up there, so we probably won't see him again, at least not very soon. The psychiatrists that I've seen all confirm the notion that I'm not unique in blaming my family. It's always there, that all patients have these episodes. Some are just more serious than others in terms of their behavior. In fact, I got the idea of the commonality of blaming the family from my doctors. They have, as a therapeutic tool, the statistics of such innocents. Lots of people have blamed their parents, so I have a statistic in my favor. From here then, I can make a new start.

So here I was in another county. The shelter I was referred to had no mattresses. At night we had a blanket to put on the floor. Every evening there was tea and bagels, and I found out about a day program. If the shelter gave me tokens, I could ride the bus to the day program. Not every day did they hand out tokens, and on the days when they did not, I walked the seven or eight miles. Usually I would get there by closing, but at least I'd kept myself busy walking. The center had lunch every day and different classes, not unlike the supervised housing. I didn't have any money, and there was only just so much I could ask from others.

It was dreary. I was given an appointment with a psychotherapist and a social worker. The therapist gave me some medication. Maybe she was a psychiatrist, because only doctors could give out medicine. I took one dose, and then threw the rest away. During one of those next appointments after this, I asked her if she could call my dad and have him drive down and pick me up.

He said was coming in a couple of days. He was going to pick me up in the morning at the medical center. I was very happy to be going home. The bare floors and the little nourishment were not something I wanted for a long time.

Dad came, and I thanked him. Since it wasn't the courts who had contacted him and needed help, I was not required to enter the mental institution. No one had requested that he do so.

This wasn't the first time I left from the house to try and be reestablished. Once I went by bus to Boulder, Colorado. It really is lovely there. I drank in the bars a lot while staying in a shelter for the homeless. The manager of the shelter warned me I was going to contract cirrhosis of the liver.

The shelter there was very nice compared to the one nearer to my home. It had breakfast with pancakes, cereal, eggs, sausage and bacon. We all slept in bunk beds that were relatively comfortable. I began to wonder about the rest of the homeless who were there. Because of my bad experiences, my mind raced when I came close to some of the Negroes there. Most people would have been comfortable around them. I, however, fantasized that they were criminals. It was, and still is to some extent, my reaction to a black person in those baggy or dirty clothes. As long as I keep it to myself, it's alright. After a long time, my emotions would pass, and I'd feel better. As the doctors would say, it will pass, and it's only my imagination.

CHAPTER 16

The mountain country was breathtakingly beautiful. There were all sorts of shops and bars. There were meetings on alcoholism, just like back in Baltimore. I attended when possible. No matter where you go, there's sobriety from people getting together to help each other stay sober. I think they even have them in Europe and Asia. The people are different, but the meetings are the same.

I was drinking one day from a brown bag containing a pint of vodka. A policewoman drove up and gave me a citation for drinking in public. The next day I went to the courthouse. All I had to do was pay them forty dollars, and I was free. I had enough money left that month to pay the fine. At this time I was in my late forties.

I usually went to a coffee and tea bar at breakfast time. I sat there with my tea on the front porch of the store where they had chairs for people to relax, socialize, and sip their beverage. One morning, I said hello to a young blonde woman there. In the midst of the conversation, she said that she was a prostitute. She also mentioned her age, which was nineteen. I believed her, and maybe she was nineteen. She could have been younger. She was very flat-chested. Her name was Ann.

A few days later I was still hypnotized by that conversation, so I left the shelter one night before it was locked up, and I went looking for Ann. She was with her Indian friend. She was always with her. I noticed her when I met Ann. After an hour or so, there they were. They had told me that they were sleeping in the park. We walked along for a little ways. Then the Indian woman said that because I had found them, I might have to make love to them. Without hesitating, I said goodbye and walked away from them.

It was getting quite cold, so I sat down in another park, not the one they slept in. Then I walked a little further, and glory to God there was someone who asked me if I needed a place to stay for the night. Now I know I would never do that for anyone if the situation arose. Then, I was quite happy to have a place for the night and not freeze to death. I told him about Ann, and I wondered if the legal age for marriage was eighteen. He said he didn't know. The very next day, I told Ann about this conversation. She really didn't have a response negative or positive.

The snows in Boulder were amazing. I was there just at the end of the snow season. It started snowing, and in ten minutes, it was snowing so hard that distances were impossible to see. I remember I was walking along when it started. I was outside during the white out. It was beautiful.

In a few days I started on the next part of my journey. I boarded a bus one afternoon in the first part of the month. I had to wait until then to afford the tickets. I was headed west to Cheyenne, Wyoming.

CHAPTER 17

Wyoming was different than Colorado. The town I got off the bus at, Cheyenne, was not developed much. The buildings even seemed to give off a sense of history. There was a small park at the spot where a famous gunfight occurred. I think it was Doc Holiday and Wyatt Earp against some famous criminal whose name I cannot remember.

The homeless shelter there was more strict than in Boulder; It was probably that way on purpose. I guess you could say that if the Cheyenne people had seen the Boulder shelter, they would have thought that it was risky and not protecting of the general population from itinerant people who might be criminals. We were required to take a breathalyzer test each day in the evening. If any of us who stayed there had alcohol on their breath, they would not be admitted.

The meals were pretty good though. Every day we had volunteers come in and fix dinner. There was even a space outside where we could smoke. I had an interview one day with a social worker there at the shelter. I told her I wanted to get off my medications. I said the pills were unnecessary for me. She said ok, and the rest of the interview was sort of plain. A few days later, it was the beginning of the month. I went to take out some money, and there was no record of my monthly deposit. I thought it was the bank's fault. I went inside from the ATM and asked about my money. I guess you could say I was disruptive, making a scene.

I finally called the agency about my money. They said they'd restore it. Later that day, it was there. I promptly got my stuff and headed for the bus depot. I think it was the social worker's fault. She must have called the people and told them I didn't need medications, so I didn't need money. After a few hours of waiting, I got on the bus and was on my way to Los Angeles.

As I traveled west, the areas of land always changed. The west wasn't as wild. At first the biggest difference I noticed was a sort of Mexican flair to the architecture. My mind imagined that we were going south, then back up at the coast to Los Angeles. I don't think so. The national borders in this particular part of the west were sort of illusory. You might as well be in Mexico, but you aren't.

We finally stopped in this area for food and to stretch our legs. The buses always stopped for about twenty minutes. I smoked and drank coffee. The bus stations at some point began having slot machines. I didn't play, but perhaps I should have.

It started seeming like we'd never get there. It seemed like we were getting there, but the bus just kept on rolling. Part of the journey it was very hot, as Spring had set in since that last snow of the year in Boulder. I didn't know how the bus was going to make it going up the hills near the California mountains. I talked to one man who was traveling by bus to visit the parks there conserving wildlife. He had been a member of a wildlife outdoors club for a long time. He couldn't have had much money because he was traveling by bus. I supposed there are all types of people.

The bus pulled in at long last to the Los Angeles bus station. It was something to look out the window and see the long awkward bus moving so slowly into the station to park. It was fascinating that something moving so fast for so many miles was now barely moving. Its long form moved delicately into a small space, which was almost exactly the size of the bus, with what seemed like only inches to spare.

It was late in the evening, so I just started walking. I was scared to death. I didn't know if I was to make it alone safely. So I finally walked up to a building that had some writing on it about alcohol treatment. They unlocked the door, and I went in.

Soon a man came down, a black man, with a large frame. He shook my hand, and we talked. I told him about my diagnosis of alcoholism and then asked him if I could stay there. He said ok, then without much more talking he took me upstairs. The room he said I could have was nice. A window was open above the bed, blowing soft spring air through the room. It was very pleasant, and I put my stuff there, a duffle bag. I went around and talked to some of the men, then I went back to my room and slept.

I dreamed of mother and Stan, my stepfather. They were attending a party in the Hollywood area in the dream. Of course they weren't, but it let me know that I was not alone.

When the morning came, I left the Samaritan's alcohol place and went to find a more conventional homeless shelter. This one was architecturally similar to jail.

How did I know what a jail looked like inside? Well I've been arrested twice. There was only one conviction though, which was hitchhiking. Also I've visited jail to speak to inmates about alcoholism. Sometimes the people at the meeting place back home I mentioned where we talk about how to stop drinking, go on visits to alcoholics in prisons and in institutions. The theory is that if we do that, it will help a great deal for us to stay sober. The mental image of the disaster that has occurred to a human being due to alcohol use is helpful to prevent us from drinking. No matter what the deterioration is, the individual must see how there is benefit to others.

These alcoholics who are inmates in jails do help show us a warning not to drink. Their lives are this warning, and they are valuable to others as such. It is also is a theory of alcoholics that if a person who is qualified as a alcoholic drinker, he or she will always eventfully end up in jail, the hospitals or in mental hospital. So these guys in prison are to us simply alcoholics who could not stop drinking and drank to the point that they would do anything to keep drinking.

I used to go to the bar across the street and drink all day. After leaving Cheyenne, I didn't have any more trouble with my disability payments.

The line was forming along the wall to enter the next homeless shelter I found. One of the fellows there sort of looked at me and growled. I was afraid he'd steal my money. Instead he sort of backed off; I guess he was worried that the police would pick him up because he was so close to the homeless shelter and its staff.

After staying there for a few days, I was offered a job working at the shelter. I started thinking about it, and decided to buy a bus ticket back to Towson, Maryland instead.

The next day, my duffle bag and I were on a bus home to Maryland. It took about four days. We stopped in Las Vegas and other stops, but only for a half an hour tops.

Bus riding was a wonderful adventure. Ordinarily, I'd never get the chance. My family flies for long distance trips.

Well soon enough, after I failed to show up for my disability hearing, they had scheduled another appointment to determine if I was still eligible for my disability payments. I didn't believe that the whole thing was necessary. I believed it would last forever, and the appointment was ok to be ignored. Shortly after the date of my appointment, I received a letter stating that my payments were going to stop again. I wondered what I was doing to do. After a few days I decided I would go to the emergency room and see if they would admit me to the mental hospital.

After walking through the sliding doors of the emergency room, I approached the nurse on duty and told her I wanted to go to the mental hospital. She asked me if I was suicidal. I told her about my hallucinations and how fearful they were. After ten minutes of her processing my request, I was told to go into the treatment room. I was hungry and asked for food. They found a turkey sandwich.

I had to wait about two hours until a psychiatrist showed up. He asked me various questions and left. From then it was just a matter of waiting for the ambulance to take me to Spring Grove, a Baltimore county public hospital. There were certain procedures to be followed, including the long drive to the hospital. When we arrived there, the ambulance driver pulled me out of the doors of the ambulance and put me just beside the door of the Dayhoff hall. I was still tied to the stretcher. This was the ward where I would be staying.

About forty-five minutes later, the Dayhoff office was ready for me. The drivers and paramedics unfastened me and took me to the front admitting room. The lady there asked me a lot of personal history and identification questions. Then a nurse from the Dayhoff D ward came to take me in. We went through a series of locked doors until she finally unlocked Dayhoff D.

It was a wonderful hall. It was October, so there were all sorts of Halloween decorations on the walls. They showed me to my room first. I didn't bring any clothing except for those on my back, since I knew the hospital provided clothing. I was even there in time for the evening cigarette break. So we all walked into the inner courtyard for a smoke.

You couldn't get out of the inner courtyard without climbing, since the walls were very high. This way it was easy to let us smoke. We could be outside with no risk of patients going AWOL. I started talking to the other patients. They were of various ages. There was even one rather pretty girl about my age.

Soon it was time for my evening medications. I did not get any, since there was a law in Maryland stating a patient had to go two days without medication until a diagnosis was made. Next was snack time, where the staff handed out juice and cookies. And finally it was bedtime.

The next thing I knew, it was six o'clock in the morning. This was wake up, where we shaved, brushed our teeth, and made our beds. Then breakfast was next. About half the hall was women. The meals were good, but there was too much food. For example breakfast consisted of waffles, cold cereal, sausage, and grits. Before long I was only eating half of what they gave us, in order to prevent myself from blowing up like a balloon. After lunch the staff hollered out medication time, and we all formed a line along the wall beside the nurse's station.

There were two stations actually. One was where the medications were given out, and one was where the records and patient cigarettes were kept. They also kept razors and various other things that needed to be locked up. Since I was just newly there, I couldn't go off the ward to the patient canteen and socialize. And I had to wait for cigarette break to smoke.

I noticed the pretty woman patient sitting at a table in the lounge. So I sat down and started talking. I started talking about how pretty she was, and how I could get to know her since we were both in the same ward. She said that would be good.

I had to keep appointments during those first two days. The psychiatrist needed to evaluate me. Soon I was put on medications, and I would have to stay for a while. That same week I was elevated to a level where I could go out unsupervised. The evaluation had authorized this.

The canteen was nice. They had billiard tables, television, a library, a piano, and a counter staffed by volunteers where they sold cigarettes and coffee. . I started to play billiards again too. It had been years. Every day I would play two or three games of pool, and soon I started to be fairly good at it. Not excellent, but better enough to make it enjoyable. We would be there too, everyday when the Rosie show was on. Sometimes I watched it.

Outside under a porch was the smoking area. Every day patients begged for cigarettes from those who had them. It was the same old thing, day after day. I usually said no about five times before I actually gave in and let someone have a smoke on me. If you are wondering how I got cigarettes, my family sent me money to buy them after I was established there.

I was hoping that the stay in the hospital would wipe my slate clean, and I was determined not to repeat the antics preceding the stay. This, for the most part, has done it. I only had one embarrassing occurrence that I guess I can live with. I forgot one of those proceeding episodes, so I will add it here. Hopefully the reader will not be disturbed going back like this.

I had decided one day while drinking that I would visit a synagogue across town in the Jewish section. I thought this would help my faith to see where God had started. So I took the bus and went into the synagogue.

It was different than church. I stayed only a half hour. On the way home I couldn't find the right bus stop. I was walking through a bad neighborhood too. Images of the nightmares in the inner city took over my consciousness. I started to hallucinate. I looked at the house and believed there were voices coming from them saying that Horace, one of my best friends from before I was sick, was a killer. I reported this to the police. It was very sick. Just now, some years later, I am still getting over that horrible call. Thank God nothing happened. I'm sure Horace is alright. He is a psychotherapist, so if he ever knew, he would understand it was my schizophrenia talking, making the call, not me.

I walked on farther, and it seemed like some men who were behind me were following.

CHAPTER 18

Laying in bed in the hospital, the water pipes were knocking and making noise. I could hear voices, and I believed the pipes were some gadget or another to test my sanity. Later on I thought there were snakes in the ventilator, which were going to come out and fall into my room. It was scary.

For the first time in my life I started buying Christmas gifts too. The canteen had a small room with various gifts items for sale. It was around Christmas time, and I had been there for two months. So I bought some gifts there at the canteen shop and sent them via the hospital post office. I also had long distance pre-paid phone cards to call Mom and Dad down in Florida. At this point, Mom and her second husband, and Dad and his second wife, all lived in Florida during the winter. I was a long way from there. It seems like three thousand miles between Maryland and Florida. Also here I was with hospital clothing on a locked ward with other mental patients and doctors. There was a lot of contrast.

My psychiatrist, Dr. Carter told us at a morning meeting of our ward that the best things we could all do is try to be pleasant and polite to everyone else. The pretty woman whose name was Angela started paying me attention. I had a talk about her with my social worker Mrs. Boka. I mentioned that it was not a good thing to go farther with Angela because she was married. Angela had told me about her husband.

One day later I was sitting just outside the ward on a bench, when Angela came and sat down beside me. She slid on the bench up close to me and told me that her husband was coming to pick her up. I felt uncomfortable, so I slid over away from her. Then her husband came, and she left with him for the afternoon.

Angela asked me a few days later to walk with her. We went for coffee and then found a bench. She bought me coffee and gave me cigarettes out of her pack. We didn't talk much, but I remember her being discharged, and I felt loneliness. It seemed like it was time for me to be going. A lot of the patients had either been discharged or sent to another ward. It wasn't the same anymore.

I used to like to watch television, and movies over the weekend. Also on weekends, the staff left our bedroom doors unlocked. The rooms were open, so we could take a nap whenever we felt like it. Some days it would snow or rain outside, and we couldn't go to the canteen, so we all smoked in the inner courtyard.

There was another cute girl there too, about twenty years younger than I. Any time I talked to her, she would make a big deal about it. One day she said that if I wanted to, I could be her boyfriend. At first I said yes, and she asked me to write it down in her journal. After about an hour, I started to feel very creepy. I told her I was too old for her, and she asked me if it would be a sin for us to be together. Fortunately for my sake we never kissed or went anywhere farther than these conversations. I told her yes it would be a sin.

I used to see a psychotherapist during the week, one day for about a half an hour. I used to talk about how I resented my mother because she always made me take my medications and stay off alcohol. It was just like the meetings whose source book said it was hard to accept that we were different from normal folks. It was hard to think that I couldn't drink anymore. It would be hard enough for a well person to give up drinking and even more so for an alcoholic. For an alcoholic like me, drinking was a priority. There was no such thing as stopping drinking. I liked my booze. My mother had cared about my mental health though, and for that she was blamed. I suppose she would have understood if I had told her about these resentments.

This therapy was very good for me, because I got out these feelings of resentment. The therapy goes that if one doesn't vocalize their problems, then they can build up into a severe outburst or breakdown. After a few weeks of telling the therapist about how I resented Mom's help, I was able to view these statements as unfair to her. I never could have known this unless I had therapy with Carl. He was glad to listen, and I felt more free and as a whole person, now that I had verbalized it, and it was gone.

I had another group therapy on a different day of the week with a different therapist. I didn't have much to say there though; perhaps I was not evasive, but really felt I had shared enough for a while.

We also had art therapy. We tried to put our emotions on paper with crayons, chalk, or markers. I used to draw naked women. I was getting some success with profiles and women's shapes without revealing too much personal detail.

In the art room was another pool table. Sometimes at night after dinner, we went in there and played pool. After I'd been there for a couple of months, I started going out on the Friday night van trips, too. We would go to the Baltimore arena and watch the soccer team, the Baltimore Blast. When they were out of town we went to the local community college and watched the women's or men's basketball games. It really wasn't a bad life. There is no reason to feel sorry for the mentally ill. They took very good care of us. And boy oh boy; we had professional soccer and college basketball live every Friday night. The staff did everything they could to keep us happy and occupied.

I started to develop a basis for nostalgia later on in years after hospitalization. Good old Spring Grove State Mental Hospital. I had been there before, and now this time for nine months.

The trees on the campus were very old too. While walking around on the grounds, I could see buildings boarded up and no longer in use. There were several of the closed down buildings, and only a few buildings were actually in use. The modem theories, based on breakthroughs in medication, had been experimenting with the deinstitutionalization of the patients. The new medications allowed most of the patient loads to be released to the public and to supervised housing projects. Apparently the theories were correct, because the closed wards remained closed, just as I had found them on my visits in the 1980s and 1990s as an in-patient.

I just recently received a letter from Sheppard Pratt, a leading psychiatric facility here in Maryland. It was asking for donations. In this letter it talked about how before the drug advancements were made, patients were punished for their illness. They were often, according to Sheppard, put in shackles and not really given much respect. There apparently were stigmas attached to mental illness, and this recent progress was long overdue. The letter said that it started with the "19th century Quaker social reform movement". Before this, "Mental patients were hidden away, chained in filthy dungeons, isolated, forgotten, and mercilessly punished for their sickness."

There was one thing that I found uniquely strange about Spring Grove. About fifteen percent of the patients carried around bags of instant coffee with them. They would save two liter soda bottles and mix up coffee in them, and then take it around with them. I don't know how this got started or what it means, but they carried instant coffee in bottles and bags everywhere.

In Spring Grove I discovered sitcoms too. I had never watched them before, but now every night, I sat in front of the lounge t. v. watching them while I ate dinner.

Every night I went to bed, and the pipes would always knock. They were very loud, and I kept imagining it was some sort of device meant to start patients believing in auditory hallucinations. It was like some sort of malpractice insurance, for it guaranteed patients would be crazy as diagnosed. The psychotherapists and doctors never asked me about the pipes, and I didn't mention them. I guess I was sort of lucky that way.

CHAPTER 19

My stay there was getting quite long. I had the idea that if I stayed on the ward in the mornings instead of going to the canteen, I could make it so the staff worked on my case more. Hopefully, and as I understood it, this would be the effect. After a couple of days I decided to go to the canteen anyway, even if it meant a longer stay.

One day we had an exiting time. One of the patients with epilepsy had a seizure up at the canteen. He lay there shaking on the ground. A big alarm rang out, and within minutes, the staff showed up. I think they took him off in an ambulance, but I'm not sure. There were a lot of people there, and the staff needed space, so I went inside.

Sometimes they gave out protective helmets for epileptics, so if they had a seizure they would not hurt their head when they fell. A person, when having a seizure, usually falls down.

One day I was up at Smitty's Market. It was about fifty yards away, just off hospital grounds. We were allowed there. Any one with money could buy instant coffee or a soft drink. They also sold cigarettes. Soon I was sitting on a milk crate next to a beautiful black woman with a generous bosom. Somehow I knew to steer clear from getting into any physical contact though. Nevertheless, it seemed that she was willing. She had the lock, and I had the key, but I didn't use the key. We talked about our illness and about the weather. Finally I got up and left her there alone.

On the way back to the ward from Smitty's Market one day, I found a book on the ground. It was an official book about President Clinton and his trials as a president, so I tried reading it, and it made me feel very educated and worthwhile.

They held Catholic services there at the hospital on Sundays. I didn't like the Catholic Church, but that was the only service there on Sundays, so I usually went. It was held in the geriatric building, and every Sunday, about ten old people in wheel chairs were rolled on to the lobby where the service was held. They were pitiful, very old and very sick. There were also usually about twenty other people like myself from different wards. Sometimes there were more people hanging around, just loitering outside.

In the springtime I would go off the ward on Saturdays where a league of baseball played on the Spring Grove baseball diamond. It was good fun.

My billiard playing was getting enjoyably good too. I tried new shots too. Like if a ball was near a corner pocket, I tried banking the cue ball off the near cushion then colliding it on an angle to go in the corner pocket. It was easier than shooting the cue ball directly at the ball near the corner pocket. It was hard shooting straight away to get the correct angle. When I used the cushion with the cue before hitting the ball, I was more successful. I don't know why, but it works.

When we went out Friday nights to the soccer games, I would wait for a little bit after sitting down. Then I went to the concession stand inside, away from the seats. It became routine for me to buy a couple of beers and chug them so that nobody would see. For a while I was never challenged about it.

I finally asked one of the nurses on my ward if I could get a job there. After a week or so, the canteen manager interviewed me. I got the job, however, the staff said it was getting close to discharge time. I had to cancel the job mopping up at the canteen.

Dr. Carter, when it was near discharge, asked me if I was drinking. I was an honest man basically, so I said that I had been drinking at the soccer games. She told me that if I took another drink, I would immediately be readmitted to Spring Grove.

Dad, when contacted, made arrangements to pick me up to go home. I was told there would be a meeting with the staff, my parents and I, at the time of dismissal. I was really looking forward to getting out. The hours that morning went by very slowly. I didn't have any groups to go to and no other appointments except the dismissal appointment. Finally I saw my Dad's face at the back screen door. He had his wife with him.

They were shown into the conference room where Dr. Carter was waiting for them. My social worker told me then that I could wait outside for them to be through. I was very relieved. I don't think she knew that I was supposed to be there. Nevertheless, I went outside and lit up a smoke.

After about twenty minutes, Dad and Valorie came out of the screen door and said for us to go. Apparently it was ok with the doctor that I wasn't there anymore, because the staff at the screen door waved goodbye, and we were off. Soon we were off the hospital grounds, and then after a short drive, around the city on the beltway.

Dad and his wife dropped me off at my house. I was free again, with the one condition that the hospital had arranged for me to attend a psycho-social rehab five days a week as a condition of my release. Tomorrow I was going there. I had already attended two days a week while awaiting my release, so I knew what to expect, too.

The next day, someone came to the hospital from the rehab center. It was called Dulaney Station New Ventures back then.

Now it's called Mosaic Health Services. I still attend it part-time, even nowadays.

Anyway, the person from the rehab center interviewed me, and the last question she asked was about if I had ever been convicted of a felony. I blew up and told her she had a lot of nerve. I had to apologize later to her and ask if she would come again. I had never been convicted of a felony. A few weeks later, I remembered that at the bottom of all the job applications that I had ever filled out, they always asked me to mark down if I'd ever been convicted of a felony. The woman, Beverly, had done nothing worse than every employer or job application did. I felt stupid when I realized this.

A few weeks after being released, I apologized again to Beverly when I saw her. I did not think to talk about the job applications. After that, it was too late, because the staff had to keep their distance, and it would really be too much.

CHAPTER 20

After about five months back out on my own, I drank again and stopped taking my medications. The rehab called me to see what was going on, because I missed a few days. I was required to go in and see the doctor. He said I needed to go back to the hospital. I asked him if I could go to the day hospital there at Sheppard Pratt. He said ok, but I had to stay at a halfway house on the hospital grounds until I was stabilized on my medications again.

This was a lucky break. The halfway house was not locked; we could come and go as we pleased.

I started working on ADLS. These were Adult Daily Living Skills, like showering and shaving. I started taking a shower every morning and shaving everyday also. After two weeks at Sullivan, the day hospital, I was told I could return home. I went back home and went daily to the rehab center.

After six months I drank again. It was the same routine, back to Sullivan and Weinburg House, the halfway house. I had kept up on my ADLS, so that was a point in my favor. After a month

I was sent home. I knew the doctor was giving me a break, so I started to think maybe I shouldn't press my luck. That was January the tenth. I have not had a drink since.

During this early period, I had been offered some good jobs, but my doctor said I was too sick to work. So I put work aside and concentrated on taking my medications and not drinking. I also tried to get every thing I could out of the classes at rehab. I listened and tried to do everything I was told.

I kept going to my meetings with other alcoholics about how to stay sober. Mom even bought a car that I could use to drive to meetings. This made it much more possible to stay sober. There were only so many times I could ask a fellow alcoholic for a ride to meetings.

At first it was very hard. I didn't know I could do it. I sort of just closed my eyes and told myself I was not going to drink, no matter what. Then I started to feel good and have a higher self-esteem. I needed to focus on the fact that it was the sobriety that made me feel good. If I let myself say that I felt better, and now I could drink, then I would surely drink again. I would think it was ok to drink because I was feeling well. The next logical thing then was to drink. Instead I told myself the truth. The truth was that I felt better because I was sober, and that drinking would make me feel bad again.

I think back now with four year's sobriety, that I'm really glad that my mother is still alive. We've eaten dinner together for about three years now. I'm so happy that she has lived to see me sober. It would have left a huge hole in my heart if she had died while I was drinking alcoholically. She has seen the fruit of her labor, my sobriety, to enjoy and feel good about me. It's good to know that she has been around me when I was enjoyable to be with. A practicing alcoholic is not fun to be around. It's almost as bad as it is for the alcoholic, although the alcoholic does not know it. I know that I was so miserable that I didn't even know I was miserable during my drinking years.

The theory of the meetings was that ultimately, an alcoholic cannot stay sober if he doesn't *want* to stay sober. Along with this seemingly obvious reasoning, is the idea that not until an alcoholic has "hit bottom" will he get and remain sober. I know I tried it, and I kept comparing myself out. I needed to drink until I "hit bottom". Some alcoholics have low bottoms and some have high bottoms. Some come from being locked up in jail, while others lose a job or a wife. My own bottom was personal shame. I knew from the episodes written down here, that drinking was not an option. I couldn't live with myself. Though the meetings include people who are actually mentally ill, a lot of the rest of them are at the borderline of mental illness. Their diagnosis is alcoholic, not alcoholic schizophrenia. For one like me, sobriety is crucial, because the doctor can diagnose properly only with the booze out of the patient's system. Also the symptoms are worse when a schizophrenic is drinking, so a doctor needs to see beyond the alcohol to the serious disease beneath.

During this time at Mosaic Health, I met Barbara. She was a physical fitness counselor with a degree in physical health and fitness. She had an above average bosom while still firm and shapely. She wasn't just sagging out of shape, but looked very nice for someone her age: 48 years old. I asked her if she wanted to come by my place and visit. We got there, I opened the door, and we went in. She sat on the sofa and talked for a while. Then she said there was something she wanted to tell me. I was listening.

She said she was a lesbian, and my hopes left. After a brief silence, I asked her if she was bi-sexual. She answered by stretching out her arms and welcoming me to her. Soon her blouse and bra were off, and I got my first look at those near perfect tits. A little by little, her clothing came off, and so did mine. After a few minutes, we enjoyed a passionate moment. I really didn't think about her being a lesbian. I guess I didn't want to think about it.

After a few more times together, I asked her to marry me. She said no. She did want to move in with me though. I told her we could not be together anymore unless we were married. That was the end. Her counselor told her that she couldn't have me over anymore. She blew up, and after the anger was over, her counselor told her she had to go into the hospital. Barbara never called me from the hospital, and when she was released, she moved to another apartment. I had not heard from her in months.

I remembered where she said her family worked. It was owned by her father. Her brother told me on the phone that she was living in a nursing home and could not be bothered. He also said Barbara had Parkinson's disease. Her family didn't want her place at the nursing home to be jeopardized by starting up our relationship again. I have not called her since then. I guess I will never see her again. She knows where I live, and she hasn't called yet. Today it's been two years since I've talked to her.

As for me, a few more years went by, and I haven't had a drink for almost exactly four years as I write this. It is really good for my self-esteem. I feel very secure and that I have actually accomplished something. Things don't seem so dismal. After the affair with Barbara, I started to believe that I would never again try to get married. I'm fifty-three years old, and maybe sex is for having children. If I was able to find a woman young enough, I could never give the child proper upbringing for the reason that I am poor, and I don't believe that it's fair to have a child in poverty. When I grew up I had a private school education. During the summer I went to the country club to swim and learn golf. One summer I went to an expensive camp in Maine. I always had expensive clothes. It would be wrong to have a child in my position.

During the past few years I had been sending hand written manuscripts to publishers. They sent almost all of them back. I did receive one letter from Warner books saying that if I wanted to be published, I could do so for two thousand dollars. When the letter came, I didn't have the money; I had spent it all on alcohol. If I had received it lately, in the past four years, I would have been able to publish because I have not been drinking. The question came up in my mind that perhaps this wasn't a good deal anyway, because if the publishers believed my books would sell, they would not charge anything. I had heard of this, and I believed they were called vanity publications. On the other hand, maybe this was the way all books were published, even best sellers.

When my mind started deteriorating, I began to wonder if the publishers were publishing my work, but just not counting me in because I didn't pay the fees. One time out of frustration and resentment, I wrote a letter to a publisher asking if they would give a lot of the money from my books to a woman I had seen in Time magazine. It was out of spite. Now today, I have some very bad memories of the request. I was getting better, and I could not write a letter apologizing for the request. It would be schizophrenic to apologize and to stop sending the woman money. When the bad moods strike me about this letter, I just have to sit still and hurt. There is no way out.

The meetings I attended about not drinking suggest that I make amends to anybody I had hurt. One of the counselors at Mosaic Health center, then Dulaney Station, told me that I should not worry about making amends to Time-Warner, but only to my family. I could not make amends to others here in Baltimore, but just to my family. This at first was quite a relief, but now with this I feel there is no way out. If the publishers do give money to the woman, it's like that forever. I feel trapped. At least though, I'm doing what I am told medically; I know that it is enough and don't worry. Mom told me the same thing; she said that I should not worry and definitely not write an apology.

Before I stopped drinking, I mentioned that I visited a strip club downtown. It cost twenty-five dollars just for a single beer. The girls were not like they show on TV, where the dancers have on at least scanty clothing. They were naked. I haven't been back since.

Well, that about does it for an account of my life starting when I was forty two. These days I've used what I learned in those episodes to remember that if I drank again, it would all happen again.

Like in France, where they save the salad for last, I now want to go into a little bit of what happened before, starting clear back in my childhood, that led me to drink at all.

CHAPTER 21

When I was very young, but still able to remember, I stole some beer from the refrigerator while the rest of our family was visiting another family on Maryland's eastern shore. I felt dizzy, and happy, and warm. I was hooked from that day on.

Before I could get another chance to drink again, I was taken by a fever. Mom and Dad moved me downstairs so Mom wouldn't have to climb the stairs to care for me. I kept hallucinating that the walls were moving and closing in on me. After the fever was gone, Mom wanted me to see a child psychiatrist. The pediatrician said that I didn't need one. I wish now that I had been able to see one, because of the way I eventually ended up, and maybe treatment would have been more successful.

The next time I drank was over at my next-door neighbor's house. His name was Barry, and his family owned a car dealership. They were out, and Barry and I went straight to the liquor cabinet, where we selected a bottle of sweet vermouth. After a few minutes of drinking right out of the bottle, we were getting that warm, fuzzy glow. I don't remember anything after that until I was back at my house. It was my first black out.

In just a few years, I became friends with another neighbor. He was able to come into possession of a bottle of gin every Friday night. We would buy bitter lemon or tonic water and drink all Friday night until it was gone. We usually had dates and other people at parties on Fridays too, and they usually drank part of it also.

I started to live for a drink. I started paying less attention to my homework during the week. All I could think of was that beautiful bottle every Friday night.

I had a girl friend. I started dating her when I was fourteen. Dad would drive me over to her house where we'd go down to the basement and pet and make out until it was time for dad to pick me up. By the time I was sixteen and could drive, my parents pulled me aside and said that I was not allowed to see Mindy anymore. They said the relationship was becoming far too serious for a child my age. For about a year after that, I told my parents I was going out with this private school girl I knew while I would actually keep going over to Mindy's house.

Towards the end of the year, Mindy said that we should stay home this one night while her parents were out. She led me straight to her parent's bedroom. We had talked about going all the way before, but I didn't expect that she wanted me this particular way. We petted and made out for a while, but I didn't go all the way. I don't know what it was, but I just didn't want to do it. Maybe it was because my parents had really wanted to avoid my becoming a teen father. I felt I could do that after that night, but I wanted them to trust me too. It's too bad that she did not become pregnant, because I would have ended up getting married and maybe my life would have taken a different route. If I had the power to stop, I rationalized that it was also only fair that dad and mom let me see Mindy.

After the year of lying to my parents, they found out some how and grounded me. There was no more getting blueberry ice cream out at the reservoir, and no more riding down the road with my hand between her legs. Thank goodness for automatic transmissions. No more necking in the basement could happen while listening to Dionne Warwick's greatest hits, and no more having someone to get drunk with.

After a few months, I went to a party at a classmate's house, and there was Mindy, holding hands with another classmate. Even though she certainly was justified in seeing someone else, I still took it hard. The emotional pain was awful.

After this, I didn't see her anymore except once at a class reunion where she was with her husband. She had married the classmate I saw her with that night at the party. She had two or three children by him I think.

Soon my buddy from down the street asked me if I wanted to go to another small party. I said yes of course. So that weekend we got into the car and headed for the country. It was a long drive, and I don't recall having been out there before. We finally reached the driveway. A sign was out by the gate reading Morvan Farm.

My friend pulled in, and we twisted down the long curving drive way towards the house. It was a very beautiful farm. The owner had some cows and horses pastured there. Most of it was vacant though, because the owner, Bradley, worked as a real estate broker. There were only a few guests there that night.

Right after we went in, Bradley asked me if I wanted a drink. Soon I was sitting on the sofa becoming very drunk and talking to his second oldest daughter, Pat, who was a couple of years younger than I. The rustic farm was beautiful.

I started going there every weekend. They allowed me to drink when I was there, and I was in heaven. I had all the alcohol I wanted and a girl friend to talk to.

That spring I made first string on the varsity lacrosse team. So every Friday after the game I went to Pat's house, and they asked me how the team did. The Association used to play over the stereo, along with the group Carl, Paul, and Mary. One time, just before lacrosse season, we even all rode toboggans down the ridges at the snow-covered farm. Pat had taken the place of Mindy in my heart and mind. It was very romantic.

In the autumn after I graduated, after lacrosse season and summer, I was supposed to go up north in New England to college. I had applied to Yale, University of Virginia, and Trinity College. I was turned down at Yale and accepted at both University of Virginia and Trinity. I decided to go to Trinity in Hartford, Connecticut, even though I knew I was going to miss Pat and her family. The campus of Trinity College was wonderful. Large old elm trees were growing in the quadrangle. Some of the buildings were old and historic, and some were state of the art when they were built later on after the historic brownstones. I bought all my books and started classes.

Soon I received a letter in my campus mailbox from Bradley. I was very happy at this, because no one had ever paid so much attention to me. He sent me some books that he read in college at Princeton, and I immediately started reading them and got one-third of the way through all the volumes. In three books I read all about the political climate of pre-World War Two, both here and abroad. The central character was a munitions dealer capitalist from the US.

One day a letter came to college from Bradley saying he'd like to meet me in New York. I asked him if he could bring Pat's sister with him because Pat had to be home with schoolwork. He told me that Joyce, Pat's sister, couldn't come either. I thought this was great, but little did I know what was really going on.

It turned out that he had asked me to meet him to tell me that I was not to see his daughter because I was from the wrong family. He owned horses and was very rich and did not want me to see his daughter.

Months later, Pat called, and we made arrangements to meet at the University of Pennsylvania. I had some friends there, and it made her trip shorter too. My friend was not there when we arrived, but his roommate welcomed us to stay there with him and his girl friend.

We had a big bed to ourselves. We rolled around a little bit then I left her to sleep. I didn't really think about her father much except that it was depressing. The weekend was soon over, too quickly, and Pat and I said goodbye.

At the end of the school year, I came home to Baltimore where I immediately headed out to the farm again. This time they asked me to just spend the night because it was such a long drive from the country to our house in the city. I was almost asleep when I finally got there and saw Pat in her pajamas. I woke up quick enough though when she asked me to make love to her. We did. She had grown since I had first paid her attention. Her breasts were large and shapely. They were firm enough to keep a good shape.

After that night, I would never see Pat again.

Then it was back to school again. On the way up to Connecticut, I stopped by a liquor store in New York where the drinking age for beer was eighteen. I put a case of beer I bought under a blanket so that when I reached Connecticut, it could not be seen. When I got to my room in the dormitory, it was definitely time to crack open the first beer of the case. In a couple of days, the entire case was gone.

At the beginning of the sophomore year, we were allowed to pledge for fraternity house membership, and I joined a great one. Some of the fraternities even had rooms where the brothers could live. Mine did not, but the fraternity house was very nice and new.

One of the features upon which I chose this house was that in the basement there was a beer tap. If we wanted a beer, we could just make our mark next to our name. Each mark was ten cents.

Often I would drink and end up cutting classes. We had a college rule that allowed us to take as many class times off as we wanted. As long as we could maintain our grades, we were allowed unlimited cuts. I was beginning to get out of control on the unlimited cuts rule though. My grades started plummeting. I didn't know what to do, but I wanted to drink.

When we gave parties at the fraternity house, we usually bought a new trashcan and filled it with grain alcohol, fruit punch, and some whiskey. Many times I became so drunk that I vomited. And whenever I threw up, there was room for more alcohol. My stomach allowed that.

After that year, I decided to drop out of the fraternity. Maybe then my grades would go back up. Before long however, my drinking became again a problem. The new friends drank Tequila, ale, wine, and whiskey. I was soon getting just as drunk, and just as often as before.

Before long, I was referred to see the campus psychiatrist. Upon making the effort to call his office, I had cold feet. The secretary sounded ominous, so I hung up and never called back. This was a major mistake. If I'd seen him, perhaps I would have graduated. As it was, it was not long before I dropped out of the college. I cringe when I think of all of that money wasted because of alcohol. It certainly was a shame, and it demonstrates how alcohol can ruin anyone, even at a place of success like Trinity College. You didn't have to be a skid row bum to be an alcoholic.

Towards the end, I went on a spring vacation from school to visit my brother Frank who was living in Colorado. Two of my friends from college came with me. We took turns driving and made it straight through. This was the first time I'd seen the western mountains. They were, as you would expect, awesome. Frank was living in a small mountain ski village. There were also locals who lived there year 'round. These were mainly native Americans. There were also a lot of construction people living there to build luxurious ski homes that rich families from flatter parts bought to go skiing in the wintertime.

Frank showed us around, and we soaked in the spring sunlight and beautiful mountain vistas. After ten days we started back to Connecticut where it was the same thing all over again. I was just getting by academically. I also was required to take two courses over again. When June came, the idea struck me that I should just go back to Colorado.

One of the Trinity co-eds had a boyfriend in Colorado. I also knew him. She asked if I could take her to Colorado to meet her boyfriend, and I said yes. There was a mattress in the back of my van. Instead of staying in a motel, we stopped in one of those big truck stops and slept in the back of my van. We didn't touch each other while in the back of the van. We just slept.

Soon we were in Boulder, where her boyfriend lived. He was the warden of the Boulder Jail, ironically enough. We pulled out the map and looked up the street. Soon we were parking, and Harriet and Jack, her boyfriend, embraced when we got back in. He had graduated from Trinity the year before while Harriet had still another year to go. I spent the night, and in the morning left for the mountains, just west of Boulder.

The view was gorgeous. The pass going up the Rockies to the mountain highway went back and forth, traversing the huge incline. After coming just down the mountain pass, I was in sight of Breckenridge, the wonderful mountain town where Frank had been living. Unfortunately, he had headed back to Baltimore to resume law school. I drove into town and found out where Louis and Rose, two people I had met in the spring, were living. For lack of anyplace else to go, I drove up to Louis and Rose's apartment.

They told me I could stay there for awhile. So I unpacked and then broke out the Jim Beam and Tequila. After an hour or so drinking, we decided to go down to one of the local watering holes and socialize. Everyone I had met in the past spring was there. We played billiards and drank until late. The next day I had to get up and look for a job.

The morning was breath taking. I still wasn't accustomed to all the natural beauty around me. To me it was spectacular.

One of the contractors building condominiums hired me as an apprentice/laborer. Everyone in town that wasn't a skier or worked for the ski resort was up at the same watering hole by

7:00 am. There was a restaurant in the building owned by the bar owner. Loads of pancakes, sausage, and so forth were cooked every morning. I started my days here.

I spent my whole summer working on the condominiums during the day and drinking at the bar at night. When September came, I decided not to return to Trinity and finish college. I just sat in the bar and watched the first snow. It was the first week in September. I gazed out the window and thought I'd just stay in Breckenridge. It was then that I thought life could be good without the routine of practicing law or medicine.

I didn't really know what I was getting into. It was a religious experience, the giving up of the world and its cares. All of that ambition and work ethic was absorbed by the snow and going completely out of my mind and body. Nature with all its inspiring beauty had hypnotized me. I could not get up and go back to college now.

Soon after the summer, I lost my job for not showing up one Friday. I had some money, but not much. Most of my money I drank away as soon as I made it. Winter was really coming on in the mountains during the fall of college weather. I was starting to feel vulnerable. Without employment the cold was a little bit colder, and the snow was a little bit deeper. I was starting the decline into mental illness. Things would never be the same. There would be no more parties and no more future.

Pretty soon Louis and Rose told me I'd have to go somewhere else to live. I would soon be homeless and poor. It was dangerous to be out in the cold in the mountain winter. I suppose the situation I was fast moving towards was how I became diagnosed as Schizophrenic. After months of being cold, sleeping whereever I could, it was fast becoming apparent that something was wrong. People up there knew how dangerous the winter weather was, so they offered me shelter in their homes for short periods of time. Word soon got out though that I was so sick that I was dangerous to myself. I didn't take care of myself and was in constant danger of malnutrition and freezing to death.

One day I received a phone call. Mom and Dad were coming out and taking me to dinner. I waited at the appointed time, and soon they appeared in the center of the little town. We headed east over the pass down the foothills to Denver. But instead of taking me to dinner, I was told I needed to see a psychiatrist, and they had an appointment already set up for me then. It took all the strength I had to simply go out of the car and into the doctor's office.

In a matter of minutes I was on my way to a small private hospital. The door locked behind me there, and I was not going anywhere. After two days I noticed that there was a window that had been left unlocked. One evening I simply climbed out of the window. It was a fairly long drop, but I managed to fall without breaking or spraining anything. I then hitchhiked back to the small town nearby.

I thought that was the end of it, but soon the police came and took me back to the hospital. I didn't know there were such laws. Now I did.

The most part of the remaining month I stayed in my room, reading and sleeping. Then for the last ten days or so, I had free access to the rest of the ward. I didn't leave again. It started to be nice, despite myself. I met a lot of new people, and the food was good. Then I was released to my parents. They drove me back to the town and rented an apartment for me there. After they left, it turned into one big party. I invited all my friends over.

Before long, I decided to give up the apartment and travel back to Baltimore. I was home a week, and then I was off to Sheppard Pratt, a large, long–term, private mental hospital, rated number one in the nation. It is located in Towson, just north of Baltimore city.

When I was admitted, there were rules I had to obey. I couldn't leave the locked ward except with a staff member. At first, I was not allowed to leave the ward at all.

The food was pretty good there though. It was at Sheppard Pratt that I tasted my first Rueben sandwich. Everyone who was not confined to the ward would walk over to the dining room to eat. I remember thinking that it would be wonderful to be able to get off the ward sometimes. We had hall meetings every morning at 8:30 in the morning. That was when the permission levels were discussed and voted on. I was very sleepy from the medications I was taking, and that made it hard to stay awake during the morning meetings. After the meetings I would lie back down on a sofa and go to sleep until a nurse came to wake me up and tell me that there was no sleeping allowed during the day time.

I had group therapy once a week, and individual appointments with my psychiatrist, also once a week. I was so depressed that I didn't say much. There were often long silent periods during my appointments. Things went by fairly quietly.

One time I had a roommate for a few months who was bi-sexual. He kept trying to kiss my ear. One day he ran away from the hospital, but after a few hours he was back on the ward. He lost all of his permission levels. He was back to the start.

I started playing tennis when the weather finally broke. It was the first time I had ever tried the sport. I was surprised that I was soon playing it with some degree of success, even if I had to borrow one of my hall mate's racquets. He didn't mind. Further on into the warm weather a softball team formed too. We played against local companies. It was a lot of fun.

One day I had a visitor, and I automatically wondered who it was. When I saw her, I was impressed to realize that Fran, an old girl friend, had come to see me. She was the one whom I told my parents I was dating when I was actually sneaking out to see Mindy. After hugging her, we went walking along the grounds. As casually as I could, I asked her if when she came again she could bring me some alcohol.

A week went by, and finally there was Fran again. We went off the hall, then she showed me what she had brought me. It was a two-liter plastic jug filled with vodka and cola. It was not my favorite drink, but the warm vodka was enough to please my compulsion for alcohol. This compulsion was growing stronger and stronger.

One day in a hall meeting, Bradley and I proposed a sign-out system to go into town and eat dinner. Bradley was another patient on the ward. Amazingly enough, the sign-out idea was approved. When Friday night came, Bradley and I left the hall and went out to sit on the benches out in front of the main entrance to the hospital to where the buses come. After another hour we were off.

The restaurant wasn't crowded, when we sat down and ordered drinks. After a couple more, we ordered dinner. I was whole again, and the wonderful warm, dizzy feeling was just what I wanted.

Bradley and I came back from the restaurant half-way inebriated. I thought the nurses back at the ward were bound to notice. Instead they welcomed us back, and we went to our rooms to undress and put on our pajamas.

The next day it was back to the seemingly endless appointments of therapy and group therapy. I also worked at the greenhouse. George, who was in charge, set us on tasks of planting seeds. We planted them in little egg cartons and later, outside in the garden. All different types of things we planted. The egg cartons were filled with flowers, while the outside overflowed with beans and vegetables.

After each group, we went back to the hall. The door opened, we went in, and then the nurse locked the door behind us. I was getting used to this. Even though we had been there a while, when we were on the hall, it was locked tightly.

Back then, Sheppard Pratt had a large swimming pool. We were allowed to go there on our free time to swim and play in the water. Since then Sheppard has started leasing out the pool. Patients are no longer allowed to swim at any time.

It was starting to get closer to the time of my being released from the hospital. My social worker said I could choose to stay with my father and his wife Valorie, or my mother and her husband, Stan. I chose my father. Looking back, I might have fared better if I had chosen my mother. I might have even gone back to school. However, once I made the decision, I was stuck with it. Shortly after my discharge, I asked if I could switch and go with my mother and Stan instead, but they said no.

But before my discharge, I started going on sign outs to spend the night with Dad and Valorie. There, I was hitting their liquor cabinet pretty heavily. I used to even count the seconds between weekends when I was at Dad's and could drink. The staff must have known about the drinking, but they never said anything. My depression was giving everything to alcohol. I couldn't stop. I thought that the only good thing in life was the horde. It had priority over my mental health, my family, employment, and anything else.

The soft ball games were still going on in the evening though. I really enjoyed them.

Fran stopped coming, I didn't know why. Then an old friend Alexander and his wife Peggy also came by to say hi one weekend. Betty, another girlfriend, came by also. I felt wanted. Today, it has been a long time since I've had any visitors, in or out of the hospital. Those days were a special time.

The doctor asked me if he let me go, could I limit my drinking. I said yes, honestly, at the time.

The blessed day was fast approaching. The doctors and nurses had done the paper work, and I was simply waiting until that day.

CHAPTER 22

I had my bags packed. Only one more hour to go and I would have that sweet freedom. And finally, Dad and Valorie were at the door. The nurse opened the door for them, and they came onto the ward. I was very happy to be going home. I said my goodbyes, and the three of us were off.

It was the middle of the summer time. The sun was out, with the flowers and trees blooming everywhere. While I was in the hospital, I had a girl friend for awhile who said she saw hallucinations of trees. I was glad to be out now where the trees were real. She was a very nice woman whose father was a lawyer in DC. I can't remember if he was with the government or in private practice. I didn't even get a chance to say goodbye to her because she was in a different ward from me. I was on my way.

After a few days with Dad and Valorie, Dad asked me if I wanted to go get my driver's license renewed. Before Sheppard I had been living in Colorado, so I had to change the license back to Maryland. I had previously declared that I was mentally ill, so I had to get a letter from my doctor to say I was fit enough to drive again. He did, and after a short trip to the Department of Motor Vehicles, I had a new license.

The doctor that I had, and who wrote me the letter for my license, had been referred to me by Sheppard Pratt. He was a very nice man who I was happy to be seeing.

Right after I got out I phoned one of my other previous girl friends. She wasn't there and was living in England. I asked her sister who answered the phone if she would like to go out. She said yes, and I picked her up at eight. We had a good time drinking and socializing. After we went home to her house, I talked her into having sex. I now know that I shouldn't have talked her into it. It was too fast, and I didn't know her. I needed to work on relationship skills and not rush into what would be casual sex. It was heartbreaking to fail at a relationship as soon as I got out of the hospital.

So here I had two girlfriends in the same family that I had gone all the way with. I think this was the biggest setback of my life. My behavior had made it impossible to work, and I was filed away with the doctors and lawyers as a failure. Fortunately, I was still young and had plenty of time. It would be years before I was back into a comfortable position. Sheppard Pratt was a good hospital and very successful. They were not successful with me though; I was just not getting it.

I soon had a job as a warehouse worker five days a week. It was a department store warehouse. Orders would come in for merchandise to be shipped to various retail stores of the company. I'd get the merchandise and prepare it for shipping by one of the company trucks.

After only two weeks I quit my job. I was going nowhere fast. I was drinking heavily again, and I then had a series of jobs, all of which I lost. I told my doctor that I was suicidal. It was true that I was. He wanted to put me back in the hospital and give me electric shock therapy. I really didn't want this, so I told my brother Frank who was practicing law. He backed down the doctor and found me a new one.

This second doctor out of the hospital was very nice and compassionate. He was Jewish. I would call him at his home when I was drinking and say that I was suicidal and could he please help. He repeated for all my calls the same thing, that I was not that sick and that I just needed to get a grip. I never tried suicide under his care, but it was on my mind. I was not to lose these thoughts until later, when I stopped drinking for almost two years.

He always seemed to have laughter in his eyes and was very warm and reassuring. I met only one other one like him before who saw me for one appointment at Sheppard. This new doctor's name was Lance. I think of him as a specialist with possible malpractice cases. As I wrote earlier, he kept telling me that I wasn't that sick; I just needed to be brave and enjoy life. That was just what I needed to hear too. I think he was of the opinion that sometimes, if you give someone a chance that may be risky to some, it would be worth it and helpful. I commend him because I needed to know that it was all in my mind, and it was unreal. There was nothing to be concerned with in reality.

Life went on relatively painlessly. I worked when I could, and drank a lot of alcohol. I'm sure I was in pain from drinking, but there were no new catastrophes. I did date a woman in my late twenties and early thirties who had the same last name as a cousin of mine, a cousin I had only heard of perhaps one time in my entire life. I don't remember that one time; I just know that I did meet him at my grandmother's funeral about 1996. The woman I dated denied that she was a relative. Eventually she left me. Perhaps that was for the better.

I didn't know how the drinking was bothering me. I was so miserable just from alcohol use, that I didn't know I was miserable.

After I had seen Doctor Wasserstein for awhile, the nice Jewish doctor, I was told for the first time by anybody that I was drinking too much. Dad had simply said I was drinking too much of his liquor and had to by my own. But he never said, to my recollection, that I drank too much. He might have barely mentioned it, but I just remember the fact that I was using too much of his. His philosophy was that if you could afford it, then you could drink it.

My mom told me to go to Alcoholics Anonymous, the meetings I had referred to earlier. She said that my whole personality changed when I drank, and that I couldn't drink her liquor at all. She said that I was drinking it all up. That was true.

The other stuff she said about my personality was humiliating. I did not react but swallowed my pride, said nothing much, and when I got home, I called the intergroup office of Alcoholics Anonymous. Mom knew about AA because her step father was an alcoholic too. He would go off for days on binges. Actually mom would sometimes have to go pick him up and bring him back to their farm in northern Virginia. He would drink until he had no more money and then call. Mom was convinced that I was an alcoholic, too.

There is one thing that is certain. Even if I had not been sent there to AA by my doctor, I do love and need it today. I usually think that mom got the referral for me to AA by talking to my doctor or NAMI, the National Alliance for the Mentally Ill. The intergroup told me of a meeting nearby, and I went. It was in a fashionable church room with oriental rugs and comfortable sofas. I listened. The people there were very nice and shared their experience, strength, and hopes. One thing I knew from that first meeting though. If I were to continue going to meetings, I would have to quit drinking. So I vowed never to return. After six months, I ended up in an alcohol detox with lots of alcohol education. The education was supposed to help us see the very negative things about alcohol abuse.

CHAPTER 23

Next I want to go into the actual circumstances of how I ended up in an alcohol detox. My girl friend, the one I mentioned earlier who had the same last name as my cousin, the stock broker, had been seeing another man. His name was Carl, and he worked in the emergency room at one of the local hospitals. He had heard from my girl friend that I had taken some extra pills because I was out of liquor. He confronted me with an intervention to see if I would go to the mental hospital for suicidal behavior. He told me that either I go to the Union Memorial hospital where he worked, or he would call the police. I was too sick to question this, so I went to the hospital. I can't remember if it was Union Memorial, but I think it was the one. Soon I was in Spring Field.

Spring Field is another public mental hospital. But there is a difference from the others. Spring Field will take you even if you have no money or insurance. Private hospitals take only those patients with private insurance or cash payments. I did hear once that Sheppard Pratt, a private hospital, would take Medicare and

Medicaid, but I have never been there on those payment programs. I don't know first hand whether private hospitals would actually take Medicare patients. They should however. I remember being in Sheppard Pratt, and a woman on the hall ran out of private insurance, so they transferred her to Spring Grove, another public hospital.

So here I was at Spring Field. The first day I noticed that my medication was really strong. Soon my mind thought of the fact that I had been seeing my psychiatrist, the nice one, regularly for a few years. I called him from a pay phone there at the hospital, and he said he would call my doctor at the hospital. I assume he did, because soon my medication was lowered and I was referred to the Spring Field Alcoholic rehab group. I remember hearing that after I was discharged for a month, they closed the alcohol program there.

I had been to AA before and had trouble with denial that I was an alcoholic. Now six months later, I was back in AA. However, it seems fair to say that I was in Spring Field because I believe that God was telling me to stop drinking and to go to Alcoholics Anonymous. In AA, there is the concept of the higher power, helping alcoholics to stop drinking. I feel that God, or my higher power, led me gently to His loving care and protection. The higher power can keep me safe and secure, if I listen to these big things like Spring Field alcohol rehab and take it to heart. Taking it to heart is that sobriety, or abstinence from alcohol, is necessary for me to be kept by my higher power.

As I may have mentioned here, I don't drink today. It has been four years and one month since I have had a drink. In those four years, I've only taken the communion wine at the communion rail in church, given by clergy. It's just a half swallow. After taking this a few Sundays, I even stopped taking the wine with the communion service, and just took the wafer. Though I don't consider it a drink, I do feel that it's important not to partake in the wine of the communion service.

I also drank about twelve or so, maybe twenty, cans of the non-alcoholic beer for awhile. It has 0.5 percent alcohol in it, and the label also says non-alcoholic beer on it. I don't do that anymore either. Even though I did not feel that I would drink a real beer because of it, it just seemed to me that I might be a little bit sensitive psychologically. It was in the back of my mind that I knew I was not perfect, and that it wasn't as good as complete sobriety without such beverages. It's good to have these four years and a month. I feel much more secure, and today drinking is just not an option.

When I first got out of Spring Field, I drank a quart of beer. Then I waited a month and had one more quart of beer. This is the way it went for one year. At the end of every month, I drank a quart of beer. After a year went by, my father told me that if I drank at all anymore he was going to turn me out into the street. I was a financially poor mental patient, and Dad was paying my rent. From that conversation on, I did not have a drink for one year and eleven months.

They say in Alcoholics Anonymous that a person must have a spiritual awakening, sort of like a moral reform. I had suicidal thoughts before this year and eleven months. My spiritual experience was different. I remember sitting at my desk in my apartment. I was a little sleepy perhaps, but I felt my spirit leave my body and go out into the atmosphere. Perhaps my spirit leaving is not quite the correct way to say it. I felt the worries of suicide leave my body and spirit, and since that time, I have never been suicidal again. I actually could see and feel the bad thoughts leaving me. The thought that I was sober and on my way to a more meaningful and hopefully long sobriety consumed me.

I did drink again, and my father didn't mention it. Apparently I had bought some time to drink. I did drink for a while. All the while I kept going to AA meetings. They have an expression from their main source book that says that we are, "Trudging the road to happy destiny."

CHAPTER 24

Flash to the present. Today the sun is shining, and the snow is melting rapidly. The glorious sun is so nice. It's only forty-two degrees out, but it feels like summer after the bitter cold we just had. Mom is back in her bedroom putting on her makeup for the day. I passed by the coffee she had left in the kitchen for some green tea. I am twenty-four pounds overweight, and I need to lose it, not only because I'd look better, but because extra weight is hard on the heart. Life is good being sober, and I don't want to die of a heart attack after all this. I want to enjoy each day and do what I need to do around the house.

The day after tomorrow, Mom is going back to Florida. I spent November with her down there. She wants me to go back down there and help her with things, but I don't think I will. It's not because I want to be alone so I can drink, it's just my schedule. I'm set soon to go back to work. I will work at a golf course. They give me two nearly free rounds of golf in addition to my salary.

Since Mom has started me off on playing golf again, that is a good deal.

Sobriety is not easy. No one says it is. I was sober for almost two years, and then I drank. At that point I was just beginning to "Trudge the road to happy destiny." After a time I was not drinking again. This next time it was for a year and ten months about. When an alcoholic is not drinking, he or she is usually able to function like normal successful people.

Just as I was relieved of my suicidal thoughts, I believe that everyone who stays sober receives some sort of comparable gift. For others it may be keeping or getting a job. For others it is the saving of a marriage, or getting their driver's license back. There is always something positive which happens. Of course there are also the everyday rewards of being more confident and feeling good.

I was drinking again eventually. I started to have problems again, but I was to get sober again for a year and ten months. Then finally today I have been sober for four years and one month. It's great to be alive and to enjoy life. Mother helped me along the way. Without her attention and support, I wouldn't be like I am today. I play golf regularly. I have a part time job, and I attend Mosaic Community Health Services as well as Alcoholics Anonymous. Life is good; everyday is wonderful and precious - thanks to Mom.